RETHINKING
FEMINIST
IDENTIFICATION

RETHINKING FEMINIST IDENTIFICATION

The Case for De Facto Feminism

Patricia S. Misciagno

Westport, Connecticut
London

Library of Congress Cataloging-in-Publication Data

Misciagno, Patricia S.
    Rethinking feminist identification : the case for de facto
feminism / Patricia S. Misciagno.
        p.   cm.
    Includes bibliographical references (p.   ) and index.
    ISBN 0–275–95825–6 (alk. paper)
    1. Feminism.   I. Title.
HQ1206.M547   1997
305.42—DC21   97–19209

British Library Cataloguing in Publication Data is available.

Library of Congress Catalog Card Number: 97–19209
ISBN: 0–275–95825–6

First published in 1997

Praeger Publishers, 88 Post Road West, Westport, CT 06881
An imprint of Greenwood Publishing Group, Inc.

Printed in the United States of America

The paper used in this book complies with the
Permanent Paper Standard issued by the National
Information Standards Organization (Z39.48–1984).

10 9 8 7 6 5 4 3 2 1

This work is dedicated to Vincent J. Amato, my husband and friend. His enduring support and encouragement throughout the years has made it possible for me to pursue and achieve this and many other goals.

Contents

Preface

What it means to be a feminist has become the source of much confusion within the ranks of self-identified feminists as well as those who do not identify with this term. In almost every conversation I have about feminism with either students or others outside the academy, this confusion is apparent. Whenever the question of feminism arises, the usual response is something to the effect: "I don't consider myself a feminist, but . . ." and what follows is a series of descriptions of goals, policies, and proposals that sound like feminism to me.

Despite disavowal by many of the term "feminist," the movement has had and continues to have tremendous consequences for American politics and culture. This disparity between the powerful effects of the movement and the unwillingness of so many women to identify with the term feminist alerted me to the existence of what I have termed de facto feminism. I have continued to witness widespread support for the goals of feminism among women, despite their rejection of the term feminist. This book is an attempt to shed some light on this paradox and to make a contribution to resolving it.

I come to this project after some sixteen years of research on women and feminist issues, a journey that led me through political, anthropological, economic, and social investigation to some of the conclusions reached in this book. Along the way I have gained insight, but I have also reached some deadends. These explorations have allowed me to develop perspectives as both an insider and an outsider on the debates that have come to be associated with the word feminism. These debates do not worry me in substance, as I feel all areas of women's oppression--economic, cultural, social, and psychological--need exploration, and I am indebted to the contributions of all those women who have pushed forward the frontiers of feminist research and theory.

Even with debates and divisions within the feminist community in academe and beyond, the women's movement in America shows the ability to generate support on issues like childcare, sexual harassment, workplace equality, women's health concerns, reproductive rights, and many others. Therefore, a careful consideration of the term feminist, the reasons for lack of identification with it, and the phenomenon of de facto feminism seem to be very much in order.

However, what initially strikes one about the politics against which the success of feminism proceeds is the persistent attempt on the one hand to reestablish old socialization patterns and to undermine feminism itself by appeals to "women's nature," and on the other, the attempt to place the responsibility for an alleged dissolution of the American family at the doorstep of the feminist movement. With regard to the persistence of this antifeminist movement, it would be naive to suppose that a demonstration of the contrary position would result in a cessation of these counterclaims. However, the existence of these positions affords the opportunity to establish a philosophical basis for discussing them as ideology.

It is an axiom as old as political philosophy itself that ideology is overcome by praxis, and it is for this reason that I have placed the concept of praxis squarely at the center of this analysis. Doing so has enabled me to focus attention on the experience of women on questions of identity, history, and politics, as opposed to the ideological claims about these questions. One could ask how it is that the concept of praxis is applied? This, of course, is determined by the social phenomena that are presented to us, and what is presented as a social phenomena is precisely the issue of greatest contention in this debate--that women accept the goals of feminism but do not identify with the term feminist.

The existing literature on this question provides a number of answers to this question, and this work contains some new questions as well. However, the more important question is the one that follows from it once we begin to analyze the meaning and politics that are at work in feminist identity. For, quite obviously, no matter what our answer is to the paradox of feminism (that women support the goals of feminism while not acknowledging identity with it), the question of identity surfaces in a very interesting way once we address the paradox. It is necessary, therefore, that the question of ontology be addressed as part of the inquiry into what I have termed de facto feminism. The latter is but the social expression of the paradox of feminism.

There are a number of directions one might take toward an inquiry such as the one I propose. One can, for example, examine the various ideas that women have about what constitutes being a feminist. Or, one can focus on consciousness-raising as it is expressed in survey research and attempt to construct the factors that go into the transformation of consciousness--the exposure to role models, attendance in women's studies courses, and so forth.

Another method is to approach the question of identity directly and to focus on feminist ontology through the use of the phenomenological method. Using praxis to accomplish this seems particularly appropriate given the topic of this inquiry--women's political action against the backdrop of ideological constructs that are largely bracketed by de facto feminists.

Studying feminist ontology by using this method requires that the issues that initially present themselves--the political and historical reasons why women do not identify themselves as feminists--be examined first. It is only after we have provided answers to this question that we are in a position to address the ontological question of identity, because it emerges from the process whereby we analyze the politics of de facto feminism. The philosopher Georg Wilhelm Hegel sometimes referred to this aspect of ontological analysis as the labor of the concept, or as referring to the general idea that the parameters of inquiry should emerge from the inquiry itself.

This book is arranged according to this method, and so the question of ontology and identity is addressed in the latter chapters. Initially, the task is to set out the reasons why women do not identify with the label feminist.   Therefore, I begin the analysis by sketching out in the Introduction the general outline of the work. Chapter One focuses on the historical reasons why women have not accepted the term feminist. The chapter examines the early issues raised by feminism, and establishes the countermovement position regarding the traditional role of women in society. Chapter One is an examination of feminist history, and while it is an account that places an emphasis on women's praxis, those who are already well versed in this area may wish to focus on later chapters.

The historical examination of the seeds of divisiveness brings the issue of sameness and difference to the forefront of the analysis. When we discuss the source of divisiveness among women, we are focusing on the issue of role-change itself, which, as Joyce Gelb and Marian Palley noted in their work (1978), continues to be the area of greatest tension between and among competing political visions of women's future.

The analysis of sameness and difference in Chapter Two raises the importance of specific social structures such as the family and marriage, since these have long been known to inform perspectives on sameness and difference. But the analysis of sameness and difference also dictates a need to focus on the socialization process from the point of view of politics. The structural and institutional dimensions of the political socialization process constitute the subject matter of Chapter Three. Specifically, we examine the process whereby women's socialization is initially confronted by their praxis. For this reason, then, Chapter Three marks the beginning of the analysis of the political conflict between de facto feminist praxis and patriarchal ideology.

Our analysis is continued in Chapter Four where feminist identity is viewed from the perspective of this same praxis, and where the discourse on identity is seen as following from, rather than determining, de facto feminist praxis. Chapter Four also outlines the philosophical basis for the understanding of the transformational self and should be of interest to those concerned with conceptions of the self. One important feature of our study involves moving beyond merely stating or depicting feminist praxis toward an exposition of the political economy that supports and reinforces the development of de facto feminist praxis. This is undertaken in Chapter Five where the needs of de facto feminists are stated as expressions of political needs arising from the contemporary political economy. In addition, by focusing on women's activity in the political economy, we are able to raise the important political questions that de facto feminists by their very existence pose.

Chapter Five also marks the beginning of the analysis of the ontology of de facto feminism, as we stated earlier, since the questioning of feminist identity can only take place once a space has been cleared by establishing the parameters of the political, economic, and sociological structures that delineate asking the identity question.

The first step in assessing de facto feminist ontology is the reconstruction of the different contributions that developed from the earlier stage of the analysis. Once we have established the connections between history, politics, and sociology, we are able to provide the context for assessing the meaning and points of reference of de facto feminist praxis as it relates to ontology. This reconstruction takes place in Chapter Six, and makes the case for viewing de facto feminism as a relational ontology whereby de facto feminists establish their praxis against the backdrop of a political and social condition--the feminization of poverty. Finally, in Chapter Six, we also approach the question of class and de facto feminism. We attempt to show how the theory of de facto feminism meets the twofold objections of abstraction and determinism.

In the Conclusion I emphasize the transformational role of de facto feminism as leadership. Here, the grassroots activities of de facto feminists, both in history and in contemporary politics, offer a competing version of social change when looked at from the point of view of leadership, from those of elite accounts that stress the individual, and exceptional qualities of leaders.

Acknowledgments

I would like to give special thanks to John C. Carney (New School for Social Research), my longtime friend, for the valuable suggestions he made during the writing and editing of this work. His keen philosophical insights at critical junctures made a significant contribution to this work. I would like to thank H. Mark Roelofs of New York University for editorial contributions to earlier versions of this work. I would like to mention John Peeler and Amy McCready of Bucknell University who read earlier versions of this work and also made valuable editorial suggestions. I would also like to mention Robert Pecorella of St. John's University, who gave his support at the idea stage of this work.

This work could not have been written without the interactions I have had with the students in my Women and Politics courses at Bucknell University and Manhattanville College. I would also like to acknowledge the support and contribution I received from the late Mary G. Edwards, my friend and adviser. Her commitment to women's studies has served as a powerful role model for my own work. Lastly, I would like to thank my husband, Vincent J. Amato, gifted writer, for valuable editorial support throughout the writing of this book.

Introduction

The point of origin of this analysis is the paradox within contemporary American feminism in which many women who agree with (and, in many cases, actively support) the goals of modern feminism refuse to identify themselves *as* feminists.

This creates problems for contemporary feminism on both the theoretical and the practical levels. On the theoretical level, the problem arises because the analysis (including the language and concepts) that many feminist scholars employ often serves to alienate the women they are supposedly trying to represent (Stanley, 1990). On the practical level, the problem is that organizing to bring about policy changes that affect the everyday lives of so many women can be frustrated and even rendered ineffective if women do not identify with the organizations that are grouped loosely under the banner of "feminist."

Therefore, an analysis of the term *feminist* must be undertaken to determine what it is about that term that makes so many supporters of feminist goals unable to say, "I am a feminist." Thus, the curious phenomenon has developed where women will begin statements in support of a feminist position with the familiar phrase, "I'm not a feminist, but . . ."(Black, 1989; Conrath, 1990).

This is a significant problem for feminism inside the academy and beyond. Feminist scholarship has evolved in the past two decades into a voluminous literature with a very sophisticated level of analysis. It is hoped that by studying the question of feminist identity from a praxis perspective that a greater emphasis will be placed on the commonality of political struggles and thereby avoid overlooking a greater number of women who support feminism, but who, for reasons I discuss in this book, do not accept the label feminist. A narrow perspective on what it means to be a feminist has led to an increased pessimism over the chances of success for feminist positions, a pessimism that may not, in fact, be warranted. The problem is also significant because it limits the opportunities for promising scholarship based on the efforts of a much larger population of women than is now recognized as feminist.

The solution to this paradox may involve several theoretical and conceptual changes in how one thinks of feminism. Some of the categories of feminist analysis may have to be rethought and new categories added. Some fundamental assumptions may have to be questioned before an answer to the question, "What does it mean to be a feminist?" is achieved, enabling us to view feminist identity within a historical context. I want to explore the way in which posing this question sheds light on the meaning of feminism and identity.

BACKGROUND TO THE PROBLEM

The question of what it means to be a feminist has been lurking under the surface of a great deal of feminist thought. Understandably, many analyses have tended to emphasize the particular ideological perspectives of feminism that the authors thought needed further explication (e.g., liberal feminism, radical feminism, socialist feminism, and, most recently, cultural, maternal, and some postmodern feminism). While these analyses remain vital to the study of feminism and provide powerful insights into the root causes of women's oppression and inequality (and provide possible vehicles for eradicating women's oppression), there continues to be a need for an overall approach to the question of feminism per se--what is the meaning of feminist identity? Therefore, in many regards, this study will be breaking new ground. However, there *has* been some scholarship that is extremely useful in leading up to the focus of this analysis.

One interesting issue, an issue that may serve as a point of origin for our inquiry, comes from the collection of essays entitled *What Is Feminism?* (Mitchell and Oakley, 1986). In her lead article, Rosalind Delmar correctly identifies the problem with many definitions of feminism. She further identifies the struggle among disparate theoretical and ideological positions that have become entrenched with each claiming to be *the* one true feminism (Delmar, 1986). She further raises the question of feminist unity and whether unity should be an expectation of feminism at all.

In this way Delmar comes very close to asking the question posed by this analysis, but she does not ask it. She accepts that there is a problem in modern feminism and she describes and explains it. However, she misses the larger phenomenon: The problem lies not only within feminism and with self-proclaimed feminists, but also with a larger population of women who support the goals of feminism yet either outrightly reject or simply do not identify with the label feminist. Ultimately, this involves the question of identity per se, for these women have traditionally not been counted as feminists.

Midway through her article, Delmar ponders a question that alerts us to the need for a phenomenological analysis. She begins by asking the question: Can someone be a feminist by her actions? Raising the question in this way has led me to examine the relationship between identity and politics and the end result of that inquiry is this analysis. It is our precise contention that there is a large population of women who do not explicitly identify themselves as feminists but whose praxis makes them what we will term de facto feminists.

When we discuss the question of feminist identity, it is important to note that there have been several important contributions to the identity side of this question, and here Denise Riley's work (1988), as well as some of the recent work of Jane Mansbridge come to mind. However, what this analysis wants to focus on is the relationship between identity and politics--the structures, institutions, and political forces that enter into the question of feminist identity when viewed from the perspective of praxis.

Another body of literature that has had an impact on our study concerns itself with feminist consciousness (Cook, 1989; Conover, 1985; Gurin, 1986). Feminist consciousness studies are important to the analysis because the history of the feminist movement depends upon consciousness-raising as a vehicle for educating women. Even more important, most studies of who is or is not a feminist have historically relied on studies that measure feminist consciousness. Therefore, feminist consciousness studies will be analyzed to determine what role feminist consciousness actually has in defining a feminist. It is the contention of this analysis that consciousness studies leave out de facto feminists who may not fall into the particular categories that have been used to define feminist consciousness.

Another area of emphasis for the study will be the label "feminist" itself. Nancy Cott's etymological study of the word feminist raises the possibility (although it is not made explicitly as a connection in her work) that the women who do not identify themselves as feminists do so because of the ideological interpretations of the word itself (1987). Perhaps Cott doesn't make this connection because she maintains a definition of feminism that adheres to the problematic notion of explicit identification with the group called "women," as primary and pivotal.

Many de facto feminists may not explicitly identify with the "group called women." Further, it has been argued by some that feminism to a certain extent represents an attempt to escape things traditionally female. This notion of identification is difficult for de facto feminists for complex reasons, which Patricia Gurin addresses in her article, "Women's Gender Consciousness" (1986). Our study will address the structural elements of female socialization.

There have also been a number of popular studies addressing the question of who is and who is not a feminist. A series the *New York Times* (Dionne, 1989) launched over a decade ago set the pace for a continuing examination of this question using survey methods. Susan Faludi (1991) and Naomi Wolf (1991) as well as Paula Kamen shed light on this question. Some of these will be introduced to examine their contribution toward an assessment of what popular factors and conditions serve as obstacles to women's identification as feminists.

Hopefully what emerges from these phenomenological considerations is an initial awareness of what it means to be a feminist. In so doing, we need to provide a more complete analysis of consciousness studies and the ideological divisions that exist among feminists. The idea is to provide a more inclusive and positive approach to what it means to be a feminist. The objective of this phenomenological inquiry then, is to provide *a praxis* perspective on what it means to be a feminist and thereby to formulate what feminism would look like if it were to be constructed from the bottom up. The connections that exist among feminist identification, ideology, consciousness, and women's material conditions in the United States need to be situated within a more complete theoretical understanding.

THE THEORETICAL APPROACH

Many of the popular accounts of feminist identity have noted the negative connotations that have become affixed to the term feminist by the media and by misinterpretations of what it means to be a feminist. However, while these help to explain the currency of the problem, these explanations are far from exhaustive.

Before proceeding it may be useful to note some of the reasons for these negative connotations, especially since we will be examining them in future chapters. The literature, for example, suggests that there is a strong relationship between how the word has evolved historically and its present negative status. There are also structural reasons for the lack of a feminist identity that are relevant to de facto feminism. These include the socialization process, as well as women's role in, and relationship to, the family; but, they also include such factors as one's relative degree of autonomy and labor force participation. These issues will be analyzed as well.

The analysis will proceed on two levels. One will examine history to discern the manner in which feminism became defined along increasingly narrow lines (as an ideology requiring a "code of conduct"). The other level of analysis will focus on the structural developments related to women as a group--social roles, increased labor market participation, levels of higher education, and political participation (Mueller, 1990; Gelb and Palley, 1978). Here the literature clearly points in the direction of key societal institutions, such as the family (Gerson, 1985) and work environment, as well as economic circumstances. These structures will be examined in order to understand what it is that mitigates against feminist identification.

Finally, it should be noted that in attempting a reanalysis of feminism from the perspective of feminist identification within a context in which feminism as an ideology is itself a problem, an important *theoretical* issue arises--How does one prevent the very undertaking from becoming what it is attempting to redress? And that is the problem of abstraction. However, by reestablishing the historical and ontological contexts from which these diverse phenomena were abstracted, the difficulty of abstraction should be avoided. This should be the case since abstraction consists precisely in the failure of an analysis to reconnect historically connected phenomena in their political, economic, and social contexts.

Barbara Bergmann (1986), Gerson, and Mueller implicitly provide an additional safeguard against this difficulty. Their works in focusing on women's *activity* as opposed to ideology are paradigms for an analysis that is based on praxis and human agency. By studying feminist identity on the basis of praxis and agency, we are referring, in the former, to activity that is either devoid of ideology or is less self-consciously ideological. In the latter, we are referring to what Carol Gould calls "the capacity for choice" (1988: 111).

Because the work focuses on praxis as the basis of analysis, it may be useful to provide a brief history of the term and the sense in which it is used in the book.

PRAXIS AS A POLITICAL PHILOSOPHY OF SOCIAL CHANGE

One of the ways in which political theory has attempted to account for social change is through the concept of praxis. The word itself, of course, has its origin in Aristotle, and specifically in his distinction, Arendt tells us, between poiesis and praxis. Where the former term denotes makings things, the latter includes activities such as theory.

It is not until Rousseau, however, that the concept of praxis is used to explain political and social transformation. It may be useful to recall that in the *Second Discourse*, as in *The Social Contract*, Rousseau grounded legitimacy in that process whereby the individual in a state of nature, isolated, appetite driven, and barely intelligent, is transformed into a willing and willful member of a community. It is in this process that the individual becomes a moral citizen, effecting what Hegel will later term a *leap in being*. Hegel made use of praxis both in his extensive analysis of the history of philosophy, as well as in the formulation of his social theory.

Marx's analysis, as has often enough been pointed out, reflects the contribution of Hegel, and this is certainly the case with his use of praxis. It is Marx however who gives praxis its contemporary form. He used it explicitly to explain the labor process, where, as he puts it, "both man and Nature participate and in which man (woman) of his (her) own accord starts, regulates, and controls the material reactions between himself and nature. He (she) opposes himself (herself) to nature as one of his (her)own forces, setting in motion arms and legs, head and hands, the natural forces of his body, in order to appropriate nature's productions in a form adapted to his (her) own wants. By thus acting on the external world and changing it, he (she) at the same time changes his (her) own nature" (Marx, 1977: 177). Here, the emphasis is on transformation. However, it is on a kind of transformation in which the interaction with nature is guided not only by the reason of the individual actor, but by the reason that has been incorporated into the materials at hand, or the means of production. It becomes a model of how everyday life unfolds or develops. It also means that labor per se is the primary model of this process.

We come finally to the important distinction between "practice" and praxis. The distinction traces to Hegel's concept of experience where thought experiences itself as reflected, or as self-consciousness. It is a two-fold process where consciousness experiences itself as forming the quality of experience as well as being informed by the selfsame process. "Practice" on the other hand can simply be the rote performance of an activity, as in some forms of production in which there is but the single direction of activity to consciousness, and not the two-fold process noted in Hegel.

There are a number of other approaches to praxis, notably that of Sartre and Arendt, and while both view human activity as not reducible to a behavioral model, there are considerable differences between them. The anti-behavioral aspect of praxis, or the ontological component in it, is sometimes glossed over in discussions of theory and practice, where praxis is often used in such a way that it is indistinguishable from practice. The consequence of this is that "praxis" sometimes comes to stand for little more than "making things." The last position is untenable for those who approach the question of praxis from an Arendtian point of view, for whom "making things" could hardly be further removed from the actual meaning of praxis (Dietz, 1990).

Finally, with regard to "practice" itself, an important exception to the positivist meanings associated with it is that of Foucault, for whom practices, since they are the ways in which the self is constituted, are ontological. They are so, however, not only because they are the way in which being is constituted, but because, as technologies of the self, they intersect with other technologies thereby giving rise to other meanings of being (Foucault, 1993: 203).

NOTES

1. The distinction between "practice" and "praxis" is an important one that traces to Hegel's concept of experience where thought experiences itself as reflected and is an expression of freedom. It is a twofold process where consciousness experiences itself as forming the quality of experience (subjective) as well as being informed by that same process (objective). "Practice," on the other hand can be simply the rote performance of an activity, as in some forms of production in which there is simply the single direction of activity to consciousness. There are a number of different approaches to praxis, but the most important ones with regard to this paper, are those of Sartre and Arendt. What they share in common is an antibehaviorist approach to human experience. In particular, both Arendt and Sartre stress that human activity is not reducible to patterns of activity that are extrinsic to the individual. This nuance in the concept of praxis is sometimes glossed, and praxis is sometimes used in such a way that it becomes indistinguishable from practice, in which case praxis comes to stand for little more than "making things." This latter position is untenable for some who approach the question of *praxis* from an Arentian point of view, for whom "making things" could hardly be further removed from the actual meaning of praxis (Dietz, 1990).

2. Marcuse notes the connection here as owing to Hegel's ontological concept of labor. As he put it, after drawing the points of distinction between Hegel and Marx: "The basic concept of Marx's critique, the concept of alienated labor, does in fact arise from his examination of Hegel's category of objectification, a category developed for the first time in the *Phenomenology of Mind* around the concept of labor" (Marcuse, 1983: 13).

3. Labor, of course, for Marx as well as Hegel, is not only a concept that refers to "work," but to the creative process by which human needs are fulfilled. A Hegelian or Marxist would note that the actual negative connotations that have accrued to the word "work," and their distinction from a creative process of expression, are in fact the precise measure of alienation.

Chapter 1

Historical Perspectives on the Origin of Feminism and the Seeds of Divisiveness

The seeds of divisiveness in the women's movement began inauspiciously with the origin of the popular understanding of the term "feminist," a term that came, in time, to mean whatever its speaker and listener chose to make of it. From these inauspicious beginnings, the initial and apparently not very important lack of clarity over what is meant by feminism has burgeoned into a situation where women today are decidedly at odds with what constitutes feminism, what the feminist agenda is or should be, and what it takes to be identified as a feminist. This situation has a profound philosophical and practical impact on the ability of women to develop, support, and enact a true feminist program that addresses the commonalities of all women.

The term feminist came into popular usage between 1910 and 1914 in the United States. Prior to that the activity in support of women's rights and equality was called the "woman movement." The "woman movement" existed in the United States before the term feminist was accepted (Cott, 1987:3-14). The term feminist actually originated in France. It was picked up and used by American women without much reflection because it was already being used by newspaper articles to describe their activities. Thus, in a very important sense, the term feminist was coined by the popular media and was subject to all the vagaries of identification and definition of any popularly coined phrase.

However, at the time, there was value in the adoption of the term as it was presented by the press. The automatic usage of this term allowed women's rights advocates with very different agendas to either accept or reject the term as helping or inhibiting them. In essence, the term provided them with a starting point for self definition and the definition of their agendas. However, just as the term suffragist (which became ridiculed and saw suffragists reduced to being described as "bloomer girls"), espoused a number of different philosophical and political positions, the term feminist began to have widely divergent attitudes, beliefs, and even methods of dress ascribed to it. This was most notably a result of early feminists' analysis of sexuality and the institution of marriage.

Early feminists, consequently, were ridiculed as advocating free love, for example. The popular press and the conventional thinkers were able to color contemporary perspective because of the lack of any rigorous uniformity in the understanding of what feminism actually espoused. The variety and range of implied and explicit issues associated with feminism, especially as it was understood contemporarily, made acceptance of feminism difficult for many women and made it fraught with deep emotional conflict. This was less the case with suffragism, which ultimately could be looked at in terms of a single issue with a foundation in the interpretation of law and due process (although the experience of suffragists *also* helped to enhance the divisiveness within the feminist movement). In effect, the popular mind took hold of the term feminist, and used it according to the divergent and contradictory objectives and positions of anyone choosing to interpret and reinterpret "what feminism is." With each interpretation and reinterpretation, women were excluded or excluded themselves from solid identification with the movement as a whole.

HISTORICAL ASPECTS OF THE SAMENESS AND DIFFERENCE DEBATE

What is important for our analysis is that this situation allowed women's groups with fundamentally different and often contradictory perspectives to identify themselves as feminists. It also discloses the beginnings of a debate that continues to exist within feminism today, a debate that makes it difficult for many women who might identify themselves as feminists to do so. In essence, this debate can be understood in terms of sameness and difference. It has been referred to under different terms by many feminist scholars. Simply put, the sameness and difference debate can be described as arguments for equality based on women's "sameness" with men, and arguments for equality based on women's "difference" from men. These different perspectives have been the cause of much confusion and difficulty, both among women who have problems identifying with the term feminist, and among self-identified feminists. Generally, those who argue for equality based on sameness state that women are the same as men--fully human--and are entitled to the same rights and freedoms as men. Those who argue for equality based on difference state that women deserve equality so they can celebrate their difference from men--a difference that implies, in some cases, a higher moral nature, and, in others, an outright superiority.

It is essential for our analysis to understand these categories of sameness and difference because many of the contemporary debates surrounding feminism and feminist analysis are still founded upon this philosophical problem. Important for our analysis is that one of the potential stumbling blocks to feminist identification is de facto feminists' perspectives on issues that stress differences in areas such as traditional female behavior, attitudes, and, in general, the expression of femininity. This is the initial reason why the sameness and difference argument figures largely in this analysis and it will be discussed in more detail in the following chapter and further developed throughout this analysis.

Another area of confusion surrounding the term feminist in the early Twentieth Century (as well as currently) is based on the equation of the struggle for suffrage and equal rights with feminism (in other words, the equation of a single issue with the entire meaning of feminism). Nancy Cott (1987) makes the critical distinction between the suffrage battles and the feminist movement that encompassed a much broader tradition including the earlier "woman movement."

Importantly, the conflict between single-issue politics and broader-based definitions of feminism has contributed to the reluctance to embrace the concept of feminism and of women to identify themselves *as* feminists. Also, it is in the context of a larger social movement involving many specific social issues (and not a single, historically specific issue) that we are defining de facto feminism and within which we will locate de facto feminists. From this perspective, feminism does involve equal rights--but it also encompasses much more than equal rights. Therefore, for our purposes, we will distinguish between feminism as a larger social movement and its organizational form (Ferree and Hess, 1985:1). For example, the National Organization for Women encompasses both organizational groups and unorganized (and usually indeterminate) numbers of followers within which are found de facto feminists.

Looking at feminism as a larger social movement that is able to include many expressions of feminism helps to refocus us on what feminism means and has meant throughout history, beyond the individual moment. It also provides us with a concept and definition of feminism that is inclusive rather than exclusive and that "opens up" the field of feminist inquiry to more than just legalistic issues. It is important to note that: "Social movements raise serious questions outside normal government channels, often concerning subjects which are not being treated as topics of political concern" (Costain, 1980: 100).

This all-embracing and ontological concept of feminism has been present from the beginning, even when popular misconceptions of feminism (as we have seen) were making it difficult for the mass of women to identify with feminism. It is in this sense that the early feminist movement can best be understood.

Early feminist activist Carrie Chapman Catt (at a time when suffragism was at a peak and many thought of the woman's movement only in terms of the vote) defined feminism in 1914 as "a world-wide revolt against all artificial barriers which laws and customs interpose between women and human freedom--an evolution, like enlightenment and democracy, with *no* leaders, *no* organization, and local variance in its specific objects" (Cott, 1987: 15). This definition is a good illustration of that larger understanding of the movement. Catt's quote implies a broad, ever-changing, and ever-responsive action-oriented agenda for what ultimately is women's freedom ("a revolt"). In this context, the new feminist movement necessarily had broad appeal to women who were organized and women who were not. It implied a movement much wider than the suffrage movement without demanding universal acceptance of all of the goals and points in the agenda. In this sense, it is important to see how this concept of feminism related to the early and popular image of feminism and how the goals of suffragism related to a more expanded sense of the movement.

There was a distinct difference between suffrage advocates who saw the vote as sufficient and those who regarded it as little more than a crumb. To feminists:

the vote was only a tool. The real goal was a complete social revolution: freedom for all forms of women's active expression, elimination of structural and psychological handicaps to women's economic independence, and an end to the double standard of sexual morality, the elimination of sexual stereotypes, and opportunities to shine in every civic and professional activity.(Cott, 1987: 15)

This agenda implied radical changes in every aspect of women's lives, especially their lives in the early Twentieth Century. As one might imagine, there were those who were willing to sign on for some but not all of the agenda (even among those who could cut through the murky popular image and see the issue in its broadest context). Popular culture also worked against the acceptance of the feminist ideal. It is worth recalling the circumstances of women at the time who were in many instances legally, economically, and socially dependent upon their husbands, a condition dictated and approved by prevailing social norms and mores. Beyond this, it is well documented that women's roles as wives and mothers, living almost exclusively within the household sphere, were defined socially and morally as "natural." Therefore, it required a considerable amount of courage to challenge the existing structure of a patriarchal system with such significant social pressures allied against them. It is, in fact, all the more surprising that the feminist movement, broadly speaking, survived at all. However, it did continue. Yet, the social and moral pressures, augmented by the uncertainty of what exactly feminism was, caused ever deepening divisions, which continue to this day.

It is the contention of this analysis that despite these divisions and differing definitions, there was and is a common thread connecting feminism at its origin and feminism now. The thread is the passion and drive for human freedom that transcends the moment and that gains its strength (from the First Wave to the present day) from the understanding of feminism as a larger social impulse (Ferree and Hess, 1985:1). The validity of this contention is underscored by the fact that feminism as a social force is still a vital one despite the resolution (or lack thereof) of a series of single issues and changes in the popular image. There is something in the human spirit and sense of justice that continues to give feminism its vitality and relevance.This quest for freedom took the form of negative freedom in the First Wave of feminism in the drives to gain freedom from legal and formal restraints (the lack of the vote, property restrictions, disfranchisement in all forms), and positive freedom--the drive to actualize women's full potential economically, socially, and politically in the Second Wave.

In the so-called First Wave of feminism, Carrie Chapman Catt's description of feminism notes that feminism will take diverse forms depending upon the historic particularities of the day: "In Persia, feminism is a demand for education; in Turkey it is an attempt to unveil; in China and India the crying demand of women is to substitute a free choice of husbands (Cott, 1987: 14). Freedom then, for Catt, was the very essence of feminism, and it was both universal as well as historically specific. It is important, then, to trace the quest for freedom at that time and its impact on the feminist movement.

Early women's rights advocates had to overcome both formal, institutional barriers to freedom as well as informal ones. With regard to women's freedom, suffrage was an essential step--but only one step--in a continuing process. Other victories included the reform of property laws. The informal structures that worked against equality for women were extensive in the later part of the twentieth century and were often codified into the formal ones (Schneir, 1972: 72). Here one thinks of the notorious example of patriarchal attitudes that were written into the legal codes of the day, and in fact, one can see in Blackstone, the influential legal scholar whose textbooks were widely used at the time, an example of this. In the latter's *Commentaries on the Laws of England*, he notes "the husband and wife are one person in law; that is, the very being or legal existence of a woman is suspended during her marriage, or at least, is consolidated into that of her husband." The first changes in property laws took place in 1848 and asserted, among other tenets that, "the real and personal property of any female who may marry--shall not be subject to the disposal of her husband--and shall continue as her sole and separate property as if she were a single female" (Schneir, 1972:72).

While property laws and legal concepts may have been the institutional form of these structures, the overall system that brought these laws into being, patriarchy, also needed to be addressed. This raised the issue of tactics and strategy, and early women's rights advocates were careful not to raise radical proposals for fear of jeopardizing the suffrage effort (an early example of how the need for organizational consensus to address a single issue mitigated against the drive for a universally understood and accepted concept of feminism).

However, the attempt to quell disunity for the sake of suffrage success could not stop debate. Many of the debates over the value of special female legislation (based on difference from men), as opposed to strict adherence to equality on the basis of sameness with men, raised exactly these complex issues concerning women's equality. The essence of the debate became this: Was inequality remediable through the law or did it require something approximating a sexual revolution? Thus, even in the apparently unified attempt to achieve a specific political victory, the internal tensions caused by lack of agreement on what constituted feminism could not be controlled and spilled over into the public arena. These early debates among the mid-nineteenth century women's rights activists were not only concerned with specific legislation, but broader concerns as well. We can see this in the Seneca Falls Declaration where, even in 1848, the issues surrounding equality were broad, and some of the remedies were, in fact, radical.

The history of mankind is a history of repeated injuries and usurpations on the part of men towards women, having in direct object the establishment of an absolute tyranny over her--the law, in all cases, going upon a false supposition of the supremacy of man, and giving all power into his hands. (Schneir, 1972: 76).

The lack of a commonly accepted definition of feminism, its nature and goals, led inexorably to dissension "in the ranks" and brewed controversy and conflict among those who favored one approach or the other. This situation, incidentally, helps to dispel a revisionist history that equates the early feminist movement exclusively with suffrage. The fact that these debates *did* exist points out that the popular image of feminism *as* suffragism was erroneous, although to many (including women unwilling to consider the implications of feminism as social revolution) that easy and relatively comfortable equation was the definition of feminism.

Suffragism as a single issue and a rallying point for the *woman movement* and early feminists had, as we already briefly discussed, an enormous impact on the increasing divisiveness within the woman's movement. It was a successful campaign. Yet, its success exacerbated the conflict between women, leading to internal conflict and philosophic polarity. With the vote, women who enlisted for the single issue (and who had come to see the women's movement and feminism simply in terms of suffrage) dropped out of the movement, especially when it became uncomfortably clear to them that many of their sisters actually saw feminism as revolutionary. Similarly, women involved not only in the suffrage struggle, but who were also interested in the broader aspects of feminism, saw the struggle having to necessarily proceed to the next step--a step that required a more radical approach and a more radical philosophical foundation.

It is within this context that the argument over sameness and difference took shape. The more radical feminists in the First Wave of feminism identified the patriarchal family as the source of women's oppression and called for changes in women's place in the family and in the institution of marriage itself. The broad coalition that existed and led up to the vote experienced philosophical and tactical divisions. In many regards, these divisions represented the de-coupling of a broad base of women supporting the suffrage movement from their more radical allies and were the first hints of political conflict within feminism. That radicalism, concerned primarily with freedom, included a broad attack upon the inequality found in the institutions of marriage and the family. That even early feminists, who in the popular mind were associated strongly with suffragism, thought of the movement as more than a single issue effort is borne out by the position of people like Elizabeth Cady Stanton. Throughout the suffrage struggle, Stanton held the position that suffrage did not get to the real issue for women. It was her view, as well as that of others, that it was chiefly in the institution of marriage that the cause of women's oppression was to be found.

Many of the more conservative members of the women's rights movement, including men, were loathe to even consider this question. Consequently, Elizabeth Cady Stanton often commented that when the issue of the family was raised it was as though a raw nerve was touched, such was the acrimony to a critique of the institutions of marriage and the family (Schneir, 1972: xvii). Her recollections on the matter are telling:

No words could express our astonishment on finding, a few days afterward [the Seneca Falls Declaration] that what seemed to us so timely, so rational, and so sacred, should be a subject for sarcasm and ridicule to the entire press of the nation. With our Declaration of Rights and Resolutions for a text, it seemed as if every man who could wield a pen prepared a homily on women's sphere. All the journals from Maine to Texas seemed to strive with each other to see which could make our movement appear the more ridiculous. (Stanton, 1898: 131)

Stanton would become even more radical in her critique with the bitter defeat of suffrage, at the state level, in Kansas. She took the view in the aftermath of that defeat that men, by virtue of their socialization into patriarchal attitudes, were incapable of assisting the cause of women's liberation. The notion of equality of the sexes was so far from even being entertained seriously by most men that, Stanton contended, only women could relate to the injustices that sprang from this inequality. Stanton, in effect, was arguing for women's sameness with men in a context where women's difference was the dominant idea. Such a position, of course, did not endear Stanton or her colleagues to women who supported suffrage. Many of them did not see the issue in such extreme terms, especially when the strategy for the vote was often based on sameness.

When suffragists were attempting to gain the vote they could stress the sameness argument, namely that women's entitlement to equality was to be found in the natural rights arguments based on the Declaration of Independence--an argument that, despite its novelty at the time, *could* be embraced by people well situated and comfortable within the prevailing social and moral system. As suffragists argued for the individual right to participate in the development of the laws that governed them, they stressed their similarities with men (Mueller, 1990: 285).

Yet suffragism *was* a radical movement and its eventual broad-based support clearly points to the fact that women, when they saw the legitimacy of the idea, were not adverse to throwing off conventional constraints and moving en masse toward a common (and revolutionary) goal. In support of this, Carol Mueller points out that this demand for full equality was a radical demand in the late nineteenth and early twentieth centuries. Then it was seen as an important precursor to freedom in all areas of women's lives (Marilley, 1989: 29). In fact, this historical tendency to argue for equality on the basis of sameness with men found its expression in both the first drive for an Equal Rights Amendment (ERA, 1927) and the second drive (the ERA in 1976). The argument that women were the same as men, and not some inferior species, was the argument that was emphasized in both efforts and, in a *general* sense, was widely accepted (although issues such as women in combat, sharing rest rooms, and the question of child care and support continue to plague those espousing the sameness approach).

A competing strategy that continues within feminism is to argue for equality on the basis of difference. In this view, women are spiritually, culturally, and emotionally different from men and should be given full empowerment to express this difference. A critical aspect of this argument during the First Wave was that for women to raise the moral fabric of society, they needed the vote. This competing strategy was used simultaneously in the battle for suffrage with the arguments for sameness. In fact, in Nancy Cott's view, the arguments stressing women's "natural" higher moral character and their greater concern with social issues (i.e., temperance) gave them unique qualities and enabled them to make society more humane and moral.

However, the difference argument could be a double-edged sword. Cott describes strategies *against* women based on difference.

They focused on the roles and identities of women as members of families more than as individuals; they premised their social policy on the observation that women were weak or vulnerable; they believed one had to treat the world as it was now, a world of sexual inequality. Florence Kelly wrote eloquently in this view from 1921 that: "So long as men cannot be mothers, so long as legislation adequate for them can never be adequate for wage-earning women; and the cry Equality, Equality where Nature has created Inequality, is as stupid and deadly as the cry Peace, Peace, where there is no peace." (Cott, 1972: 56)

These arguments centered around whether, in the achievement of equal rights, women would, in fact, lose protection that had been hard won by socialist and labor groups working in a broad coalition at the beginning of the century. This coalition was now being split over the issue of sameness and difference. After years of turmoil the suffragists embarked on a strategy which enabled them to agree to disagree on everything except getting the vote (Marilley, 1989: 29). In that, they were successful. In forging a common concept of feminism that dispelled tension and division, they were not. And that tension and division remains today.

Within the women's movement, sameness and difference remained a source of internal conflict. It can be argued that the division over sameness and difference remain one of the reasons why women did not succeed in the passage of the ERA in the 1970s. In fact, some feminist activists in the 1970s were split over whether to support the ERA over the same issue--the fear of losing the protective labor legislation that women had won earlier. However, it is clear that the Second Wave of feminism in the United States generally continued to stress the sameness or equality argument. In fact, Carol Mueller, citing Anne Costain, writes "that of the eight original demands of the National Organization for Women, the four most far-reaching concerned equality; the four more narrow and specific, women's special needs" (Mueller, 1990: 288).

The fact that the 1970's feminist movement was passionately committed to the sameness perspective is reflected in its concentration on the elimination of sex-role stereotyping and its aiming for what could be called an androgynous perspective (H. Eisenstein, 1983: xi).One can recall the emphasis on uni-sex dressing, uni-sex hair cutters (as opposed to barbers or beauticians) and switching household roles, with men for the first time staying at home with the children while the women worked outside the home. All of these were outgrowths of this perspective. The theory behind this praxis was clearly sameness. Women and men are the same therefore, one can do anything the other does, and attempts at keeping women tied to sexroles, which were now understood as socially constructed, were useless. It is imperative to appreciate the full significance of this emphasis on sameness in the Second Wave of feminism because, as a political tactic for passing the ERA, it fostered exclusivity and was considered "socially dangerous," a tack that the new right used in their campaign of fear and antifeminism.

The emphasis on sameness can be contrasted to what finally occurred during the successful suffrage campaign in which the suffragists used both arguments--sameness and difference--to "divide and conquer" the opposition, creating a haven for people of all perspectives and inspiring cooperation across the board (if only for that one issue). This might have been an effective strategy in the struggle for the Second Wave ERA because research has indicated that people were not opposed to ERA specifically but, due to fierce campaiging by antifeminists and the New Right, were made to fear a radical change in gender roles and the family had it been ratified (Marilley, 1989: 26-27). Once again, the popular image of "what feminism means," and the rhetoric of many feminists themselves, helped drive a wedge into the potential broad base of the women's movement and tended to replace possible cooperation with often bitter divisiveness. Rather than dividing and conquering its opposition, the leading and most vocal elements of the 1970's feminist movement were themselves divided and conquered because of a lack of clarity about what they ultimately espoused and the ideologies that frightened (or were made to frighten) the nonideologically oriented.

However, despite the defeat of the ERA, women did make significant gains with the feminist agenda during the 1970s by stressing sameness. Anne N. Costain notes that:

By the early 1970s equality became the main focus of congressional action on women. An egalitarian majority in Congress passed bills to give women equal access to credit, to open military academies to women, to put women on federal juries, to allow girls to play Little League Baseball, and to equalize benefits between male and female employees. (Costain, 1990: 160).

This phase of the movement was necessary to shift society and women's consciousness from an acceptance of woman's lot as "natural" and "biological" to a recognition of these ideas and roles as socially con-structed. In this way, a further distinction was made between sex and gender.

However, this process posed threats and existential choices for women caught in what Kathleen Gerson calls "unequal social change," because arguments for equality based on sameness called into question the traditional housewife, male breadwinner scenario. This has caused a rift between women who support women's rights broadly, but remain situated (and comfortable) in the traditional pattern (Gerson, 1986: 213).

This made feminists susceptible to the efforts of right-wing antifemin-ists who were interested in portraying feminism as antifamily. Even while feminists were analyzing women's work in the home with the intent of exposing it as real work as opposed to the then dominant notion of it as a natural "labor of love," these efforts were being seriously critiqued. Right-wing groups exploited these analyses and played upon the fears of the longtime traditional housewife by suggesting that the feminist movement was going to force them out of the household, stripped of rights and protection, and push them, unprepared, into the workforce.

Generally downplayed by society at large was the fact that it was feminist groups that were uncovering and trying to highlight a situation that long existed (and which statistics bore out): that many longtime homemakers, after years of work in the home, were left with no support when their husbands left them in later life, in effect, facing the same dire situation they feared would occur if the feminist agenda was accepted. Also, it was the women's movement that had the category and concept of "displaced homemaker" accepted, and that influenced and pressured public policy to provide training and other assistance to women in this situation.

Despite these achievements however, right-wing pressure groups were more successful in their use of media tactics designed to exacerbate fears regarding the ERA. These tactics ultimately proved successful because they tapped fears that existed even in the First Wave and made these fears a major part of the then evolving public understanding of what feminism was. In the media, the right was successful in identifying ERA supporters as "women's libbers" which, in turn, they defined as antifamily and antimale. Thus, all the negative, rhetorical, and erroneous connotations of "women's lib" became fixed in the public mind as being the essence of feminism. This was almost an identical repetition of early women's rights advocates being termed "freelovers" and being identified as antifamily.

The fact of the matter is that in the Second Wave during the 1970s, the women's movement was *not* as narrowly defined as the Right and the media often portrayed. In actuality, the feminist program was wellfounded in the overall movement for liberation and started as a program for the liberation of women in the 1960s in conjunction with the Civil Rights and antiwar movements. The "language of liberation," of course, *did* figure prominently in the movement, but it certainly was not the *entire* movement (H. Eisenstein, 1983).

It is important when discussing the context in which the Second Wave of feminism emerged to recall the distinction made earlier--that the social movement encompassed at any one time the organized women's movement. In fact, the feminist movement was a larger movement and did contain the more radical women's liberation movement. In an attempt to bring large groups of women into the movement, the feminist movement faced similar problems in the Second Wave to those of the First Wave. The same divisions that existed in the early "woman" and suffrage movement emerged in the Second Wave when the more radical members of the women's liberation movement accused the women's movement in general of becoming too accommodating, too mainstream, and of abandoning the language of liberation (Hartmann, 1989: 65). These same charges had been leveled at suffragists for not attacking male privilege and marriage.

A more careful analysis reveals that although the mainstream women's movement may have abandoned the language of liberation, the ideals of freedom still comprised its unspoken agenda both then and now. We can begin to see here why explicit identification with the term feminist is so difficult, in view of the confusion that exists and has existed in the popular mind over what feminism actually represented to women. A part of this confusion stems from identification of feminism with the leaders of the feminist movement. Therefore, it is important for our analysis to make a distinction between the larger women's movement and the vanguard of the women's movement.

History tells us that in any social movement it is the vanguard who will espouse the most radical aspects of the movement's program, while the larger, unorganized elements--although supporting the movement and carrying out parts of the program--will, at any given moment, reject some parts and embrace others. In fact, the women's movement enjoys widespread support, while feminists who are out front as something of a vanguard are considered too threatening. Later, we will examine this again when focusing on how the term feminist enjoys less widespread support even while the larger women's movement and the goals of feminism are widely accepted.

This raises an interesting paradox for contemporary feminism but one that also provides an opportunity for change. While feminists might refer to feminism when writing in one context and the women's movement when writing in another, there is a basic understanding that the ultimate goals are the same: changes in the position of women, the granting of full equality, working toward a more integrated society. There is, however, in the popular mind, a distinction between "feminist" and the "women's movement." In fact, Naomi Black quotes a Gallup Poll citing 85 percent of those women polled crediting the women's movement with improving the position of women in the past five years. This indicates support and acceptance of the women's movement even while these women did not identify themselves as "feminists." It seems clear to say that a number of these women prefer to say "I am not a feminist, but . . ." and then support equal pay, freedom of choice regarding reproduction, and any of the many issues that have involved women's actions" (Black, 1989: 10). In the popular mind, feminism has come to mean "radical" or "militant" because of the more extreme position taken up by the more outspoken representatives of the feminist movement.

When arguing for total equality or sameness with men, the most threatening issue is that of personal relations. Feminism's insistence that the "personal is political" left many women struggling with male dominance and patriarchy on an individual level, without providing them the social supports to back up such efforts. The most problematic of these is the critique of relations within the family. Because this problem exists in the so-called private sphere, where women traditionally have been consigned, analysis of this area calls into question what is many women's only area of identification. Further, it calls into question the role of women in the household and, in many cases, their identity as household manager, mother, and child raiser. The feminist demand for child care to allow women to work outside the home was a double edged sword-both liberating and frightening. It was liberating for some women who needed child care to remain economically viable. For many others, it was a frightening challenge to their identity as traditional housewife, a role that posited no need for such a policy.

While equality (sameness) won victories in the public sphere (equal pay, etc.), special protection based on the traditional role (difference) was being questioned (e.g., child custody, child support). Ann Snitow comments:

Willingly or not, activist lawyers find themselves pitted against each other because they disagree about whether "equal treatment" before the law is better or worse for women than "special treatment," for example, in cases about pregnancy benefits or child custody. Should pregnancy be defined as unique, requiring special legal provisions, or will pregnant women get more actual economic support if pregnancy, when incapacitating, is grouped with other temporary conditions that keep people from work? Should women who give birth and are almost always the ones who care for children therefore get an automatic preference in custody battles, or will women again lose more ultimately if men are defined by the law as equally responsible for children and hence equally eligible to be awarded custody? (Snitow, 1989: 213).

Thus, the historical debate between sameness and difference is evidenced in recent feminist theory as well as in feminist practice. While the Second Wave has relied more heavily on the "sameness" argument, it must be mentioned that recently there has been a renewed trend toward the difference perspective. Several hypotheses have emerged as to why this has occurred. The most compelling is articulated in Hester Eisenstein's work (1983) where she refers to the "reactionary tendencies" present in the difference argument. The analysis is even more compelling when one considers the 1983 publication date of her book, prefiguring a then emergent, and now growing trend in feminist scholarship.

Essentially, difference theorists want to celebrate women's difference (whether biological or socially constructed), such as a nurturing impulse or a higher moral character. This has spawned concepts such as women's spirituality and women's culture. This perspective runs counter to the sameness perspective, particularly in regard to gender roles: "instead of an elimination of gender-distinctions, women-centered (difference) theorists want to celebrate these" (Eisenstein, 1983: xi). The reactionary content of these ideas, as evidenced by Eisenstein, Dietz, and Stacey, lies in their ability to isolate women and move them back into the private sphere. It led, inexorably, to philosophical conflict. H. Eisenstein notes that in the 1970s,

women were being encouraged to overcome the defects of feminine conditioning and to seek to enter those areas of public life previously closed to them ... the nature of the patriarchal structure that oppressed women went virtually unmentioned. In part as a reaction to these developments, the view of female difference from men begin to change. Instead of being considered the source of women's oppression, these differences were now judged to contain the seeds of women's liberation. (1983: xi)

This perspective has led difference theorists into arguing for traditional female values and, in some cases, a return to traditional private sphere activities. This split within feminism over arguments for sameness and difference is important for this analysis because it again raises the issue of the family, an issue never fully resolved by First Wave suffragists because of their fear of losing the ballot struggle. The inability of feminists to deal adequately with this issue stripped of its ideological trappings continues to plague feminism and to provide antifeminists with fuel for the fire.

Therefore, the seeds of divisiveness that were planted during the late nineteenth and early twentieth centuries over what feminism means and what constitutes the feminist agenda have borne fruit today in the ideological debates and conflicts over sameness and difference, the popular image of feminism, and the need to define feminism and the feminist agenda in such a way that all women can find a place within that construct, regardless of their philosophical orientation.

Chapter 2

Feminist Identity and the Contemporary Sameness and Difference Debate

Nancy Cott, in discussing the use by early suffragists of sameness and difference as a political strategy noted that suffragists were as likely to argue that women deserved the vote because of their sex--because women as a group had relevant benefits to bring and values to defend in the polity--as they were to argue that women deserved the vote despite their sex (Cott, 1987). An excellent illustration of sameness and difference as a strategy in the suffrage movement is the suffragists' decision to align themselves with the issue of temperance. As Cott points out, suffragists made their argument for the vote strongest when they showed how it could impact upon the drive for temperance, an issue based almost exclusively on difference. Temperance, after all, grew out of the debate over women's assumed superior moral standing and consequent, almost metaphysical, responsibilities.

In fact, throughout women's struggle for equality, it often appeared that the sameness and difference issue was itself nothing but a strategy. When suffragists were attempting to gain the vote, they could stress the sameness argument--that women's entitlement to equality was grounded in natural rights arguments--an argument that could be, if not embraced, then at least accepted, by even those who emphasized difference.

Many of the analyses of sameness versus difference as a strategy highlight the manner in which it has served to constrain public policy dialogue and de-emphasize the decision-making process in public policy areas. The question that arises is: What exactly is it then about the sameness and difference debate that makes it so problematic?

Although the sameness and difference debate is a focal point of analysis in this chapter, this is by no means an attempt to provide a comprehensive overview of that debate. In this chapter, I will make the case that one of the difficulties with sameness and difference in the contemporary period is the subtext that it generates concerning "human nature." At one level, the very fact that both sameness and difference were successfully used as political strategies to gain the vote should underscore the incompatibility of essentializing either sameness or difference with the historical record of women's pursuit of politics. The case needs to be made that the problem with sameness and difference is structural and that underlying it is an epistemology that is unverifiable because it is ultimately based on an abstract conception of men and women--supposedly established in an antiquarian past as "human nature"--forever to guide the hermeneutics of gender. Yet, precisely because sameness versus difference is an unresolved question, the use of praxis to study the recent history of the question of sameness and difference should highlight the theoretical pitfalls of these arguments. On the other hand, the effective use of sameness and difference seems to underscore the reality of *intentionality* in feminist praxis, and the central role of freedom that is latent in these arguments. To that end, I use the contemporary example of the Sears Case ("the sex discrimination suit brought against the retailing giant by the Equal Employment Opportunities Commission in 1979, in which historians Alice Kessler-Harris and Rosalind Rosenberg testified on opposite sides") as an illustration of a praxis approach. The case was noteworthy for the fact that it raised many of the difficulties surrounding sameness and difference (Scott, 1990: 138).

It is useful to note that sameness and difference as a formulated strategy and as a perspective on social relationships itself has a history. In contrast to the ironclad distinction stretching infinitely into the past that it appears to be, Carol Lee Bacchi (1990) makes the point that it did not come into existence until the early years of this century. Nineteenth-century women did not question the overall sexual division of labor, and one could argue that it was only *after* the establishment of property rights and the issues that lay on the horizon of the post-suffrage political milieu that sameness and difference would become established principles for informing public policy debate.

The ideological contortions of the Second World War years, when women were first encouraged to sameness and then later reminded of difference, underscore not only the heavily imbued social construction of sameness and difference, but also the flexibility of women in dealing with these dramatic, though by no means unique, ideological conflicts.

Politically, the conflict often took the form of debates over protective labor legislation and equal rights, although it is also important to note at this juncture that this political conflict was more often than not exploited by opponents of women's rights in order to exacerbate conflicting social divisions, such as those between women who work in the home and those who work outside the home. For example, comparisons of the opponents of feminism in the First and Second Waves stress the similarities in the arguments used by both, as well as the use of fears surrounding sameness and difference (Marshall, 1991; Marilley, 1989). Much of this is writ large in the 1970's attempt to win passage of the ERA (Mansbridge, 1985).

However, these liberal equality struggles were also accompanied by more radical proposals that broke the natural link of women to the household. The Wages For Housework Movement in the 1970s was an attempt to identify, in a practical way, housework as *work*--something that was neither a labor of love nor a means of self-fulfillment for women.

In addition to the debate over sameness and difference, another development was taking place, a development that in the 1980s reached its zenith. It was the wholesale appropriation of feminist arguments for difference by ideological opponents of women's rights or social change generally. By the time of the 1992 presidential campaign this trend came center stage. In the wake of a storm of criticism leveled at the speech Marilyn Quayle presented to the Republican National Convention, where she argued that women did not want to be "liberated" from their essential natures as women, she later felt it necessary to respond to this over-whelming criticism with a clarification of her views in a *New York Times* op-ed piece. In it, she cited Carol Gilligan's work on women and *care* to buttress her assertion of women's inherent nature. This was reminis-cent of the Sears Case where feminist arguments for difference were distorted and used against women who claimed sexual discrimination.

There is something peculiar, however, about contemporary arguments for sameness and difference, something which was made apparent in many of the analyses following the 1992 Republican National Convention. It is the growing recognition that in addition to the debate over sameness and difference at the level of rhetoric, there is another, deeper philosophical debate that takes place as a subtext. Here, the debate concerns the ultimate truth claims of the nature of men and women. It amounts to an ideological conflict on the question of a "natural order" (MacKinnon, 1990; Scott, 1990). Like an artifact from the nineteenth century, it appears out of place in contemporary political discourse. It is precisely the asymmetry between contemporary, even post-modern, insistence on a politics of verification, on the one hand, and the appeal to a "natural order" as epistemology, on the other, that makes sameness and difference appear so disjointed. As Zillah R. Eisenstein puts it: "Although there is a good amount of contradictory evidence that analytically defines sex as difference--how it can be tested, what its origin is--the scientific discourse that surrounds sex "difference" continues to portray it as a unified representation of nature" (1988: 85).

The phenomenology of the sameness and difference debate is interesting because it takes place amid an argument over "human nature," on the one hand, and in a political context marked, above all, by an attack on precisely such abstract and essential truth claims, on the other. Because the "natural" argument appeals to axioms grounded in an abstract past, the arguments for sameness and difference on the basis of "nature" not only mystify social relationships, but the argument also insures that a political approach to women's rights is equally mystifying. As Catharine MacKinnon put it:

Social and political equality are lived-out social systems that are basically indifferent to abstract conceptional categories like sameness and difference. Differences are inequality's post-hoc excuse, its conclusory artifact. They are its outcome presented as its origin, the damage that is pointed to as the justification for doing the damage after the damage has been done. (MacKinnon 1990: 213)

In short, women's claims for rights or justice, considered on the basis of an appeal to "nature," cloud the political discourse as a whole. Another illustration of this is provided by Helen Lambert who captures the alienation such discourse engenders by stating: "We are encouraged to believe that compensatory action for disadvantages which are 'natural' is inappropriate" (Bacchi, 1990: 244).

The sameness and difference debate, because it casts the argument in abstract context, is not only unverifiable, but devolves into a debate over competing abstract political claims. The Sears Case is an excellent illustration of this abstract form of argumentation as it highlights the degree to which political issues are ignored in favor of a debate over the underlying assumptions of sameness and difference. It is also important to note that the avoidance of politics in favor of a debate cast in terms of the nature of women was the explicit strategy of the lawyers for Sears. This is a fact that they actually admitted--that they were able to reduce the more sophisticated EEOC (Equal Employment Opportunity Commission) perspective to a debate over the ahistorical nature of women. As the lawyers for Sears put it: "The reasonableness of the EEOC's *a priori* assumptions of male/female sameness with respect to preferences, interests, and qualifications--is the crux of the issue" (Scott, 1990: 143).

In addition to the structural flaws in the very positing of the sameness and difference argument, there are the additional ideological difficulties expressed under the aegis of sameness and difference. During mid-Second Wave feminism, for example, these difficulties often surfaced in the very language used to attack proponents of sameness and difference. Thus, women who sought role change (and thus violated the requisite degree of difference) were chided as "women's libbers." From the other side, namely difference, this ideological attack was focused on cultural feminists as "earth mothers," an insidiously sexist attack because of the one-dimensional self that it implies.

Public policy debates, intended to address specific instances of injustice, often became ideological conflicts over axioms that were antithetical to history. In a word, sameness and difference by the late 1980s had come to work to the detriment of the emergence of new feminist positions and political claims.

It is true however, that during the drive for suffrage, and even afterward, it was possible to argue that victories were won using the sameness and difference strategies. This appears to be due to the fact that as a strategy, especially during the drive for suffrage, the ultimate settlement of the issue was bracketed in order to allow women's history to proceed. Also, the ability to be able to draw on either claim was an excellent political strategy. To a certain degree it was rational, in the broad sense, to argue along such lines.

Today, however, the argument to "nature" no longer suffices to meet the needs of credible argumentation. There is simply too much scholarship in support of the claim of the social construction of sameness and difference to ignore it as the basis for discussing issues traditionally formulated as sameness and difference. The social construction perspective, however, has only served to bring into relief the degree to which sameness and difference has clouded the discourse surrounding feminist identity. The discussion of feminist identification, to the degree to which it is addressed in American politics, usually takes the form of a legal effort intended to overcome public policy that is grounded in an essentialized version of either sameness or difference. Here, the limitation of choices underscores the presence of an ideology that has made an a priori decision about human nature. The debate over available choices however, is an expansive one, and it is not limited to established patterns. We can see this in Kessler-Harris's testimony in the Sears Case, for example, when she argues that it is not enough to look simply at available opportunities, one needs to also consider the perceptions about those opportunities as well (Bacchi, 1990: 241).

In Sears, the withholding of choices was also intended to restrain human development. First, by blocking off certain patterns of action for women, Sears management and corporate culture was removing the basis for self development. In effect, such a corporate stance amounts to a form of tracking, which would likely develop certain skills and capabilities among Sears female workers while stultifying others with all the consequences of segregated and segmented skills that one would expect to find, and that some could then claim as merely a reflection of human nature.

Second, because this tracking takes place within a corporate culture that has a history, the process of decision-making reinforces existing power relationships. It serves to provide those in power with a reinforcement of the logic of their decisions since it so closely mirrors what has happened in the past.

The limitations of sameness and difference to account for the complexity of women's experience surfaced in the arguments that the EEOC was forced to rely upon. Joan Scott, for example, notes the difficulties of working within these limitations:

The irony is, of course, that the statistical case required only a small percentage of women's behaviors to be explained. Yet the historical testimony argued categorically about women. It thus became impossible to argue (as EEOC and Kessler-Harris tried to) that within the female category, women typically exhibit and participate in all sorts of 'male' behaviors, that socialization is a complex process that does not yield uniform choices. To make the argument would have required a direct attack on categorical thinking about gender. (Scott, 1990: 143)

SAMENESS AND DIFFERENCE AND TEMPORALITY

The sameness and difference debate, when viewed from the point of view of phenomenology, seems to highlight competing visions of the future. However, it also exhibits a competing set of practical political endeavors that seem to be oblivious to consequences of these arguments. The idea that such a debate is possible--where each side has at times been used to initiate practical political agendas--seems to mean that neither sameness nor difference represents an account of the self that can be viewed as essential. Instead, the very existence of the debate as a historical one seems to underscore the radical freedom that underlies feminist identity.

In place of the sameness and difference argument, which presents an abstract *past* and is ultimately reducible to an immutable "nature of woman," the praxis approach gives primacy to the future and views it as a potential. It is a potential that, through the action of the individual and group will, brings into being any number of political forms and constructs. It is here that we come to the heart of the Sears problem as well as that of the politics of sameness and difference per se.

In place of an abstract past that is unverifiable, the philosophy of praxis posits a present that initiates new issues and claims through decision making and other activities that are characterized by the fact that they are both legislative and foundational. Far from grounding the meaning of women in the past, praxis takes the very practical position of stating that the meaning of women is what women *will* decide and determine that meaning to be.

Feminist scholars have noted the consequences resulting from the epistemological grounding of sameness and difference that surfaced in the Sears case, we can see this in Joan Scott's comments:

But to maintain that femininity predisposes women to certain (nurturing) jobs or (collaborative) styles of work is to naturalize complex economic and social processes and, once again, to obscure the differences that have characterized women's occupational histories. (Scott, 1990: 145)

Among these different occupational histories, of course, are women's different class experiences. This in itself has accounted for a considerable amount of discomfort with the word feminist, as there are real differences in women's experiences owing to race and class.

It is also important to point out, however, that not only is the experience different owing to race and class, but when viewed from the perspective of praxis, so too are the qualitative needs, values, and abilities that support and follow from those experiences. The universalizing of "care," for example, may in fact be one such example where a single portrayal of women's experience is inaccurate. It might, for example, be important to ask whether a universal attribution does not undermine other, perhaps more important priorities. Keeping with the example of "care," one might want to ask if attributing something approximating a universal value like care does not undermine *individual conscience* as the ground of ethics. Certainly the problem of universalizing difference presents a number of challenges not only having to do with practical politics and strategy, but theory and morality as well.

Bacchi, in her consideration of Sears, notes the tendency of a sameness and difference approach to ignore the issue of hierarchy and cites Catharine MacKinnon asking the twofold question: "If women are in fact different, the question becomes: why has this difference been constructed as disadvantage? If women are in fact the same, the problem of their relative disadvantage and lack of power remains unresolved" (Bacchi, 1990: xvii). Bacchi, like many scholars, calls for an analysis that focuses on why difference is transformed into disadvantage as well as the institutional and structural means by which this takes place.

One of the chief concerns--concerns repeatedly expressed by both proponents of sameness *and* difference--is the way in which other important political questions go unasked under the discourse of sameness and difference. "The questions we must ask are: Why should it matter if women are the same as or different from men? Why is pregnancy constituted a disadvantage in our society? Why does the economic system reward competition and penalize caring?" (Bacchi, 1990: xvi).

We can approach this aspect of identity from the perspective of alienation. The insistence on an essentialized, or a static view of identity, and the discourse that supports it help structure the way politics are pursued and questioned. If women are viewed essentially the same as men, then the same form of alienation will exist for both genders, with the possibility that a truly critical perspective is foreclosed. If, however, women are viewed as essentially different, then their departure from the established pattern of alienation becomes the basis for being penalized.

When we examine these kinds of issues we begin to see the greater efficacy of the temporality of praxis. Because the approach of praxis is process oriented, it views change as an integral part of politics. Politically, this approach also means that emerging forms of political discourse do not suffer from an a priori bias simply because they do not enjoy the privilege of being an established category.

The need for a transformation from a strategy of sameness and difference is pressing. There are political consequences to the sameness and difference formulation, consequences that are expressed nowhere more explicitly than in the highly divisive politics that it engenders. It becomes a political conflict when each of the two principles have as their point of reference established and emerging lifestyles. Further, this political strife means that issues that require unity will be limited to the most precarious and questionable of coalitions. Seen from the perspective of difference it means accepting a definition of diversity as implying little more than the diversity of hostile, opposing camps.

Economically, the need for this change is no less pressing. In a context where the allocation of resources of society generates competition between households and individuals, claims for economic justice are stunted and seem unable to move beyond the economic formations of the past: the priority of the male norm, on the one hand, and the traditional family, on the other. Sameness and difference then, are key political components of why some women do not identity themselves as feminist. We will revisit the issue of sameness and difference in Chapter Four, where we provide a philosophical basis for the issue of identity as it surfaces in the issue of sameness and difference.

Chapter 3

Structural and Institutional Dimensions of Feminist Identity

This chapter presents an analysis of the structural and institutional reasons why women do not identify themselves as feminists and examines two of the major reasons: the confusion surrounding the meaning of the "family," and the differing ideological conceptions of feminism.

A good point of departure in any discussion of divisions and debates within feminism (including the sameness and difference debate) is the family. This owes to its emotional component and the high degree of mythology and ideology that surrounds it. When feminists and anti-feminists alike talk about the family (depending upon their understanding and definitions of the family), they are describing totally different entities. The mere mention of the "family" in America conjures up romantic images of safety, home and hearth (H. Eisenstein, 1983: 139). However, both historical and contemporary statistics indicate a picture at variance with the mythical and popular ideology of the family, especially for particular members (women and children). For them, the home, nestled in the so-called private sphere, has far too often been the source of physical and psychological abuse.

Not all the problems within the family are traceable to the tensions of modern life. The rise of what we know as the modern nuclear family was caused by an essential change in the relation of the family to the economy in the United States. Briefly, with the coming of the Industrial Revolution in the United States, work life and home life became separated as large-scale industry moved masses of workers into the factories. This took men out of the home where many had been involved in small cottage industries. And even for those who already worked outside of the home, the long hours and constant physical separation from the family necessitated by industrial labor effectively broke down ties to the home. This left women isolated in the home and created a tension between family and economy.   With this isolation came a devaluation of the work that continued to be performed in the home (Zaretsky, 1976). The reasons for this are far too numerous for our discussion here. However, one reason in particular is pertinent to our analysis, and that is that women's work in the home had the distinction of being wageless during a time when the monied wage came to be the only real measure of the worth of labor in capitalist society. That wage was now the *male* wage, earned in the public sphere, while women were consigned to doing their work in the private sphere.[1] It is true of course, that there are counter-examples of married women working outside the home. However, here we are referring to general patterns. The problem for women with this dichotomy seems obvious. The preindustrial family was considered an economic unit, the partnership and contribution of all was valued and necessary, whereas when industrial capitalism took work out of the home, it turned women who remained in the home into "dependents," relying on a male wage. This situation increased the value of male labor relative to female labor and exaggerated the hierarchical nature of the patriarchal family.

Ideologically, the mythical family became privatized, a thing removed from "real" or economic life, a haven, a refuge from the necessarily harsh demands of working life, a thing of perhaps no direct economic impor-tance, but rather the personal, private responsibility of those forming it, a social, not an economic entity (Zaretsky, 1976). The entire concept of "social" is a key ideological factor in the development of the working class familial myth. As Eli Zaretsky points out, "the nineteenth century romantic reaction to the trauma of industrialization tended to accentuate the philosophical divorce of personal existence from the negative demands of burgeoning industrial life" (1976: 59). "Society" came to represent life in categorical abstracts: work distinct from pleasure, home distinct from workplace, self-fulfillment distinct from work fulfillment. Social aspects were related to, but independent from, the economic aspects of existence. It is in this sense that women consigned to the private sphere lost all power and autonomy. Women were expected to perform all of the household labor without wages, with subordination as a rule. And all the while, they were expected to create a haven for the male wage earner.

So, when theorists glorify the family, they are talking about the "mythical" haven in the heartless world. When conservative, pro family feminists extol the virtues of the domestic sphere and the family, they are at variance with the historical reality that has (and continues to) belied the myth. The point is that the conflict between the ideological, mythical, and economic visions of the family has tended to lead many observers to predicate philosophical arguments based on incomplete analysis of the actual role of the family.

For example, Elizabeth Fox-Genovese analyzes Jean Beth Elshtain's view of the family and states:

But if Elshtain minimized the mounting evidence of the ubiquity of men's abuse of women and children within families, she does so not out of mindless denial but out of the conviction that, for most women, independence in the public sphere has offered nothing better and could, conceivably, offer something much worse. (1991: 47)

There is, however, a growing body of literature that continues to disagree with Elshtain. It should be said that the issue of the family has remained something of a sore spot for the Left in America. Many supporters, and this includes a good number of socialists and Marxists, view the working-class family much the same as they did in the early years of the twentieth century--as a bulwark against the alienation of capitalism. Consequently, their support for the family, and even the traditional form of family life, is often more vehement than even that of conservatives. It seems that the position is an odd one, for the following reasons. The socialization toward authoritarian power is very much part and parcel of the traditional patriarchal family.

The famous analyses of the family by members of the Frankfurt School dealt with the wellsprings of acquiescence to authority, and the family figured quite prominently in their analyses. Of course, there are, even within the traditional family structure, numerous counterexamples, and Elshtain draws on her own personal experiences to underscore these counterexamples. It would seem, however, that this position leaves untouched what I take to be the central issue on this topic--the pressing need to overcome the previous and historical negative praxis that is contained in the very structure of the traditional family. Women's oppression is experienced through the family because the family is the social structure that has historically been the institution through which patriarchy reproduced itself through time.

The experience of the patriarchal family in the present, to put the matter otherwise, places one in touch with the history of the institution in its capacity as reproducing oppression. For example, to take on a spouse's name is at the same time an experience of the history by which that ritual was established. When we adopt a historical perspective on the rituals that surround the family and its role in reproducing patriarchy, we quickly see that it makes little difference if one can cite individual counterexamples.

If we take the long view of history, women have barely had the time to develop themselves fully in the public sphere and are still subject to discrimination and lack of support for their empowerment. Issues such as child care, parental leave, and so forth are just making their way through the policy process. Why, for example, not just wait and give women's emergence a chance before such a swift retreat to a life that remains familiar yet insufficent?

Fox-Genovese, who is not a supporter of individualism in feminism (an individualism that views women's interests as distinct and separate from the interests of the family), nevertheless agrees that "marriage is not a viable career" and that at all costs young women must be encouraged to support themselves (Fox-Genovese, 1991: 2).

The importance of this perspective is further emphasized by the results of Ruth Sidel's (1990) stirring representation of young women who have been deceived by the old ideology of the family that postulates a "white knight," or rescuer scenario. In it, young women are encouraged to believe that they need not be prepared to support themselves because they will be cared for and protected by their "Prince Charming," in the person of their "husband-provider." These young women are lured by the dream of being taken care of while they pursue a life of nurturence and domesticity. By the time the women in Sidel's survey are interviewed, their dreams are obviously gone and they have awakened--not to Prince Charming's kiss--but to the harsh reality of poverty and desperation.

This situation is hardly surprising when one views the statistics on the feminization of poverty. The myths and ideology surrounding the family are not harmless and romantic because their consequences pose such a dramatic threat to women's well-being. In this sense (as will be discussed later), feminism is a realistic necessity for all women, including de facto feminists. The fact of the matter is that in economic terms, the family has historically been--and still is--oppressive to women.

However, this reality has been obscured by the ideology and mythology of the family. Rayna Rapp in an article notes the important political distinction in contemporary political economy between family and household. The latter is defined along lines that address its economic role in resource allocation, production, and reproduction. As she puts it, "What you get from the romance of love and marriage is in fact not simply a family but a household, and that's quite another matter." She sees families as part real and part necessary social illusion, "the function of which is to recruit members to households and mask relations of production, reproduction and consumption" (Rapp, 1982: 170).

It is Rapp's central point that the institution of the family, while "carrying a heavy load of ideology," performs dual functions and inhabits both ends of the reality-ideology pole. There is the family per se, the place where one's psyche is nourished; then there is the household, an economic unit that forms the basis of civil (and economic) society. In contemporary political economy, the relationship between family and household is an important one. In order to function as a household, certain sacrifices must be made by the family. For example, working overtime to meet economic goals takes precedence over more time with the family. Likewise, for the family to reach its emotional goals, sacrifices must be made by the household. Examples of this abound and include such things as the father or mother who says no to that all-important and lucrative promotion that involves a great deal of travel. The relationship between the "family" and the "household" turns out to be a contradiction between "culture" (broadly understood) and "economics."

As has often enough been pointed out, the way the family is structured implies, in fact demands, that women make unequal sacrifices compared to men. In addition to housework and childbearing, and child-raising, women also become the mediator between the public and the private life for the family in society. This is perhaps best illustrated in the consumer society, where women are charged with arranging the various services that maintain the household (Rapp, 1982: 175). As more and more goods are produced and marketed, the need to perform this function increases in intensity and complexity, tipping the "family" increasingly in the direction of the "household"--and increasingly creating the lie to the myth of the family as protected haven. Women's increasing burden within the confines of home and family is ironically underscored when we consider that modern material society, which is supposed to have made that "place in the home" even more attractive and safe, has actually made the home even more burdensome. The proliferation of time-saving devices for the home, generally thought to free women from household chores, has actually increased the amount of labor while only changing the type of labor--from brute physical work to more demanding and stressful "household management," and the need to manage and arrange service for these goods increases with their complexity. The nourishment/nurturing function that has always been romantically assigned to woman increasingly involves not the growth and nurturing of the family and its members, but, rather, the management of appliances and services. Simply put, the household is managed more than the family. Love and marriage, terms usually reserved for the development of the family, instead tend to be associated with the management of material households, which drive and are driven by a consumer society. An entire contemporary vernacular has developed around this relationship, which includes terms such as "household management" and "household finance."

The tension between family and household is expressed in many of the distinctions within feminism itself. When conservative pro-family feminists are defending the family,[2] they are really defending the emotional family and are expressing a retreat in many ways from the harsh realities of economic life, especially during and after the rhetoric of the Reagan years. Feminist analysis of the family and the household cannot be understood outside the needs and dictates of the economic and political system within which it must operate. Therefore when socialist (Marxist) feminists analyze women's relationship to the household, they do so to uncover the economic component of women's oppression within the home. When radical feminists focus on sex-role conditioning and male hierarchal systems, their emphasis shifts to how "those roles continued to be a major factor in keeping women from contesting their assignment to certain kinds of low-paid work, including unpaid domestic work, despite the inroads of feminist analysis into the public consciousness" (H. Eisenstein, 1983: 143). When feminists critique the family, they are providing a critique of the exploitation that takes place within the home when women's work there is undervalued and their physical well-being is jeopardized. However, they are also doing something else-- attempting to transcend in theory and practice the historical inequalities that are enshrined in its practices.

Considering the high rates of alcoholism, drug abuse, domestic abuse, and so on, it doesn't take too much imagination to understand the basis for this critique. However, as mentioned in Chapter One, an analysis of the economic exploitation and subordination of women in the family as a starting point for inducing change is extremely difficult due to all the emotional and ideological baggage the concept of "family" carries with it. No other institution has caused such divisions within and between self-identified feminists and de facto feminists than has the family. Women are socialized differently to the "family" than are men. To women, it is the loci of personal expression and an extension of their learned nurturing capacities. As Patricia Gurin points out, because women are socialized to share with and be loyal to their brothers and fathers, these interactions with men mitigate against their critique of male behavior and privilege in the family for fear of appearing disloyal. This is particularly true for working-class and African-American women, for whom the family is viewed as a collaborative unit working for the survival of all its members. Therefore, if they perceive "feminism" to mean "anti-family," it is extremely difficult for them to identify themselves as feminists.

Curiously, feminism has enabled de facto feminists to insist on more cooperation in the domestic realm, especially in two paycheck families, and to enlist men's more active participation in child birth (witness the increase in the number of men in Lamaze classes and delivery rooms) and in the subsequent parenting process.

In fact, it is in examining the family that dissension in feminism becomes most apparent. The division between household and family, and the confusion generated by the blurring of this distinction, is reflected in many of the internal debates within feminism. To a certain extent, where feminists are criticizing the family in the narrow sense described above, they are likely to be radical feminists focusing on women's oppression within the family itself (for example, the unequal opportunities open to women for self-development). On the other hand, where feminists are focused on the *household* and the strictly economic functions it performs, this analysis is likely to be either socialist feminist or Marxist feminist. Finally, where feminists are concerned with the household family relationship and woman's subordination both at home and in the marketplace (although not necessarily presented in this way), the analysis is likely to be liberal. It may be useful to underscore these distinctions and their politics in order to examine the influence each exerts separately on feminist identity. When viewed from the perspective of the family, these distinctions generate a correspondingly separate politics of the family, as we can see in Table 3.1.

Table 3.1
Political Action Orientation Chart

Agenda Setters	Agenda Examples
radical feminists	new family arrangements
socialist feminists	wages for housework movement
liberal feminists	concern with public policy issues such as maternal leave

The domestic sphere and women's activities in the family have fueled considerable debate among these ideological branches of feminism. Here we will discuss two of the most prominent ideological tendencies: liberal feminism and radical feminism. We have chosen these two positions not because they are superior or deemed more correct by the author (who, in fact, joins with a growing constituency of feminists who feels these distinctions have outlived their usefulness and obscured the greater understandings and agreements within feminism); but rather because they are the two competing visions of feminism that cause many women to not identify with feminism. The other versions of feminism-- Marxist/socialist feminism, cultural/eco-feminism, post-structural feminism-- represent different aspects of the feminist analysis of women's oppression. While some of these analyzes may prove useful to us, specifically those that deal directly with the sameness versus difference debate, to become too deeply involved in the ideological debates is to miss the point of our examination here.[3] The latter is that de facto feminists are outside of these debates and are missed by them.

LIBERAL FEMINISM

It seems appropriate to begin our analysis of contemporary feminism from the perspective of liberal feminism, not only because of the history of liberalism within which liberal feminists find themselves but because it is liberal feminism that has taken most of the criticism within the ranks of those who identify themselves *as* feminists. Liberal feminism is quite a curious bundle to unravel. Taking its cue from the liberal tradition and all it implies in the United States--emphasis on individual rights and individual freedom--liberal feminism has come under attack from the Left as well as the Right. Leftists have accused liberal feminism of subsuming all feminism under its banner. Leftist oriented (radical/socialist/Marxist) feminists feel feminism in general is too closely allied with liberal feminism and that liberal feminism has come to wrongly represent all feminism. We will examine this issue shortly, but for now we will identify the main charges this group has against liberal feminism.

Liberal feminism is charged with being short-sighted in its efforts to achieve equality based on rights and opportunities. It's accused of being overly accommodating by keeping its demands within the existing political structure and not identifying the larger structural elements that oppress women, such as patriarchy[4] and the hierarchical organizations of capitalist society. It is also accused of accepting the latter as a given rather then positing a new, more radical feminist vision of organizing society.

This vision will be different according to who is leading the attack-radical, Marxist, or cultural feminists. An interesting comment from Zillah Eisenstein highlights what she takes to be the mistaken idea that liberal feminism represents all feminism to women out there. "Liberal feminism is but one form of feminism although both feminists and non-feminists often mistakenly assume that it is feminism" (Z. Eisenstein, 1981: 6). On this point, we disagree with Eisenstein and the majority of feminists who espouse this notion. It is precisely not the case that liberal feminism is identified as "feminism" by non-feminists or de facto feminists. This mistaken notion underscores the confusion about why women do not identify with the label "feminist" even when they are engaged in feminist actions and actually support the goals of feminism. I would argue that contrary to what Eisenstein and others state, the fact of the matter is that most non-feminists view feminism not as liberal feminism, but as radical feminism. This will be addressed in more detail within the context of radical feminism, however, it should be noted here that the American media's need to focus on those points of view that have the greatest marquee value, coupled with the outright backlash against feminism within the media, means that it is the radical version that the American public sees. In recent feminist history, however, the presentation of feminism by the opponents of the ERA invoked the ideological image of feminism used by those who earlier in the century had opposed suffrage. It was culled from past efforts because it sought to present a harsh and extreme version--a caricature of feminism. The extent to which this perception exists is highlighted by the language de facto feminists use when describing their relation to feminism: "I'm no radical feminist, but . . ." Many women cannot accept radical feminism's much more ambitious and ideological agenda and do not feel comfortable identifying with a term associated with a radical perspective.

However, feminist scholars who agree with Eisenstein's assertion that feminists and nonfeminists assume liberal feminism is feminism are correct in a more limited sense, namely that many of the policies and goals de facto feminists support are more aligned with the liberal feminist agenda, including such drives as affirmative action, equal pay for equal work, equal protection, fair credit, childcare, and reproductive choice. However, while they support these goals they continue to view the feminist movement as something with a radical agenda that is militant and anti-male. Feminist political activists have been trying to overcome this image that was used by many right-wing anti-feminists to defeat the drive for an equal rights amendment. This image of anti-feminine, anti-family, anti-male, anti-homemaker fueled a tremendous debate whose repercussions are still with us today.

Yet, it is incorrect to merely reduce liberal feminism to "liberalism" and dismiss it with the same criticisms that have been leveled against liberalism for decades. Just as all socialism isn't Marxist socialism (there is utopian socialism, so-called democratic socialism, and the like), not all liberalism is the same. Liberal feminism, in fact, adds a new dimension to liberalism and parts company with it to some extent. Some have even argued that liberal feminism has the potential for the radicalization of liberalism.

This argument is made by Zillah Eisentstein (1981). There is however, one particular area, namely the family or private sphere, where liberal feminism differs from its liberal tradition and that is crucial to our understanding of feminist identification. Liberal feminists are responsible for bringing private sphere issues--so taboo in liberal thought--into the public and private sphere, and its occupants (women) into the public sphere. An example of this is the liberal feminist insistence that laws regarding domestic violence be enforced. In fact, it is the liberal feminists who insisted that terms like "domestic violence" replace terms like "a family dispute," which police felt unobligated to pursue. Previously, of course, if a women's husband beat her in her own home, it was considered a personal, not a political, problem. It was at the state and national levels that women, vanguarded by liberal feminists, argued for battered women's defense by identifying and calling attention to the battered women's syndrome and called for the setting up of battered women's shelters. Also, previously private sphere issues like child care, child abuse, and displaced homemakers were addressed with public policies, thus identifying the once individual and privatized problems as social and political problems. Liberal feminism's most identifiable spokesperson, Betty Friedan, argues that developments such as co-parenting and employers providing parental leave and split shifts for couples with children indicate that the liberal feminist strategy has made the private sphere no longer sacrosanct, as in traditional liberalism. In fact Zillah Eisenstein writes:

Liberal feminism involves more than simply achieving the bourgeois male rights earlier denied women, although it includes this. Liberal feminism is not feminism merely added onto liberalism. Rather there is a real difference between liberalism and liberal feminism in that feminism requires a recognition, however implicit and undefined, of the sexual-class identification of women as women. (Z. Eisenstein, 1981: 6)

Eisenstein further notes that:

Early liberal feminists argued for the individual rights of woman on the basis that she was excluded from citizen rights as a member of a sexual class. Her ascribed sexual status prevented her from partaking in individual achievements promised by liberal society. This recognition of women as a sexual class lays the subversive quality of feminism for liberalism because liberalism is premised upon woman's exclusion from public life on this basis. (Z. Eisenstein, 1981: 6)

It is important to add that the private sphere was also excluded from examination on a political level, leaving women in a limbo state. Eisenstein's comment concludes with: "The demand for the real equality of women with men, if taken to its logical conclusion, would dislodge the patriarchal structure necessary to a liberal society" (Z. Eisenstein, 1981: 6).

We can see that liberal feminism cannot simply be defined as "warmed over liberalism." Nor can it be dismissed as merely reformist in nature because its very essence involves subversive tendencies. Toward the end of her book, Eisenstein lists some of the liberal-feminist demands that she deems to have "radical implications." These demands were set down at the Houston Woman's Conference in 1978:

1. The elimination of violence in the home and the development of shelters for battered women.
2. Support for women's businesses.
3. A solution to child abuse.
4. Federally funded nonsexist child care.
5. A policy of full employment so that all women who wish to and are able to work may do so.
6. The protection of homemakers so that marriage is a partnership.
7. An end to the sexist portrayal of women in the media.
8. Establishment of reproductive freedom and the end to involuntary sterilization.
9. A remedy to the double discrimination against minority women.
10. A revision of criminal codes dealing with rape.
11. Elimination of discrimination on the basis of sexual preference.
12. The establishment of nonsexist education.
13. An examination of all welfare reform proposals for their specific impact on women (Z. Eisenstein, 1981: 232).

Although these demands have radical implications, they are criticized by Eisenstein for not going far enough. It could almost be said that to the extent that the goals of liberal feminism have been actualized in political practice, the future of liberal feminism has arrived.

One can see here that the confusion surrounding the notion of "what feminism is" is only heightened by the splintering of feminism. It is in this context that de facto feminists, through their actual activities "out there," actually outstrip and bypass ideology and simply do feminist things. Many of these actions will be discussed later. At this point we will turn to radical feminism and its critique of liberal feminism.

RADICAL FEMINISM

The radical feminist perspective seeks to provide for women a measure of authenticity in terms of personal choices by providing a critique of male dominance and is most identifiable as "sexual politics" (Millett, 1970). The depiction of sexual politics extends to the type of family arrangement that women find appropriate for themselves, including lesbian family relationships. This is not to say that radical feminism is exhausted by this particular platform. It has, in fact, a rather large number of issues within its analysis. It is important to note, however, that our intent is to stress the role played by the family in structuring the dimensions of feminist disunity.

The radical critique of the family has been a main feature of radical feminism as far back as the presuffrage days. Radical feminists raised the question of whether men could actually be helpful or instrumental in women's liberation due to the fact that they were part of the problem and would not easily give up male privileges. This can be seen as early as 1860 when Elizabeth Cady Stanton was drawing attention to this question, which would become an important component of feminism a century later. She noted this example after the Convention of 1860 when discussing the vitriolic opposition to women's equality by individuals who were usually quite progressive: "With all his excellence and nobility, Wendell Phillips is a man. His words came down on me like a clap of thunder--"(Schneir, 1972: xvii). As this argument developed into a critique addressing more and more areas of male domination, the opposition touted it as being antimale and, necessarily, lesbian or radical.[5] This tactic--manipulating public opinion around feminism's most vulnerable aspect--has remained a cornerstone of opposition efforts. As noted earlier, this version of feminism is also the most conducive to sensational journalism: the image of feminism portrayed on the six o'clock news is this "radical" version. Aspects of feminism pertaining to women's issues, such as abortion, child care, and equal pay, are usually presented under the more mainstream title of "equal rights," while the term "feminism" is reserved for more sensational sound bites. Lesbians and militants became the image seized upon by the mass media and were superimposed, as it were, on images of feminism. These are the images a generation of women would come to equate with feminism and what it meant to be a feminist. The exploitation of the lesbian community by the mass media has added to the reasons why many women can agree with the goals of feminism but remain reluctant to identify themselves as feminists. Nancy Cott points out (1987) that the linkage made between feminism and lesbianism has historical roots, as does its manipulation by opponents of women's equality.

At this juncture, we wish to highlight the point that the radical critique of male dominance and patriarchy in general represented a turning point in feminism, and a "turning away" in many women's acceptance of feminism. Radical analysis necessitated examining one's personal relationships, the private sphere (domestic issues), and the role of power in men and women's sexual lives. Sexual dominance, rape, and other issues were raised--issues that many in society were not prepared or willing to address.

Reasons for this unwillingness are numerous and include impressive structural factors suggested by Patricia Gurin's work on the socialization process: "the economic fates and claims to prestige of men and women are inextricably intertwined." In addition,

men and women agree on many fundamental assumptions about life and society, not only because of their common fates as husbands and wives, but because of their early socialization as brothers and sisters and the structure of their relations with other women and with men. Women's relations with each other, while frequent and intimate, are, at times, competitive. At the same time, nearly all women have, or have had, close emotional ties to men. (Gurin, 1986: 144)

As Gurin makes clear, the structural underpinnings for a widespread acceptance of radical feminism, with its emphasis on the critique of male dominance, does not exist. Instead, women's socialization provides that men are a "given."

This contradiction between the radical critique of male dominance on the one hand, and the presence and acceptance of men in women's socialization on the other, is highly significant for both the divisions within feminism and for the paradox of feminism. The radical critique of male dominance, tied as it has been to the media's portrayal of lesbianism, represents something of a "boundary situation" for many women, one that they are unwilling to cross. Betty Friedan, spokesperson for liberal feminism, blames emphasis on sexual politics for alienating many women and for diverting energy from the politics of the ERA (Z. Eisenstein, 1981). Like the issue of the family, which was discussed earlier, male dominance and the critique of it has existed throughout the period under study. It has represented a source of division for women in the 1990s as it did in the 1920s. The reasons for this situation are found again in the family, where male privilege and dominance are experienced on an individual basis and in a very personal way. This is why, when the conservative backlash against the ERA portrayed the proposed amendment as a radical lesbian-sponsored plot, they struck a chord very familiar in the history of women's liberation. It also served to mobilize the anti-feminist counter-movement in America (Marilley, 1989; Marshall, 1991). These arguments had been used before to attack women's analysis of the institution of marriage and the family. This point was underscored in American politics during the nomination of Janet Reno, whose sexuality was questioned by the media on the basis of her unmarried status. And, as if this were not preposterous enough, attorney general designate Reno had to reassure members of the media that, although she was not married, this did not mean that she did not like men.

When radical feminists attacked the inequality of the role of women in society in the late 1960s, their attacks were viewed and presented as attacks on homemakers per se and not on the institutional framework of the family. Likewise, when they attacked job segregation on the basis of gender, it was secretaries, or clerical workers, for example, who thought they were under siege by radical feminists.[6] The same was true recently when feminists tried to analyze the exploitation of women in the nursing field. Instead of blaming the male hierarchy for their situation, many nurses, felt degraded by the feminist critique of nursing.[7] In most instances, conservatives were more than equal to the task of convincing women that *other* women were attacking them and that these radical feminists were intent on having them give up their identity. This is a mirror image of something already mentioned, the case of homemakers feeling attacked when the household was criticized and, in turn, blaming feminists who were actually trying to alleviate their problems.

The requirements of the electronic media for sensational items to meet their own agendas is not our central concern here. However, what needs to be mentioned in this context is that the media's equating of the radical feminist image with feminism was decisive in the failure of some women to identify themselves as feminists and is central to the contemporary paradox of feminism generally. It was decisive because by positing radical feminism as the face of feminism it meant that feminism equals an antimale political stance and an either-or approach toward sexual orientation. The case of protestors at the Miss America Pageant who pasted dollar bills on themselves to highlight the sexual exploitation of women by the cosmetic and other sexually exploitative industries was depicted by the media as the now infamous "bra-burning" event. It was further interpreted by some women as an attack on femininity. This situation was played out again when author Naomi Wolf was attacked not only for the argument she was making, but for her own personal appearance as well. With the issues and terms of the debate framed in this way, it is certainly easier to understand why some women do not feel comfortable with the label feminist.

In the context of American politics, the label feminist is interpreted as involving radical change or militant tactics as opposed to incremental change, an approach considered more liberal. Incrementalism plays an important political role in the liberal feminist strategy to achieve legitimacy in the public mind. Joyce Gelb and Marion Lief Palley's work illustrates this point well, noting that liberal feminists are focusing on a narrow incremental strategy designed to minimize backlash and political conflict. In their article they quote E.E. Schattschneider:

It is sometimes possible to achieve significant change in the guise of incremental-ism if the importance of a seemingly narrow issue is not recognized by key political actors. . . . Conversely, the more radical the change, the more likely it is that an intense opposition will develop and possibly result in a counter-movement. (Gelb and Palley, 1978: 10-11)

We will return to this argument again in when we discuss the ontology of feminism, but for now it is clear that radical feminism represents more of a threat than liberal feminism, which appears to work within the existing bias of liberal politics. An interesting aside (and others have made this point) is that the very existence of a more radical feminism made and continues to make it easier for liberal feminism to achieve its goals (Gelb and Palley, 1978: 363).

In any case, what has evolved has been a consciousness by women who do not consider themselves to be feminists because of the fear of identification with radical feminism. Also, because of this, many women see feminism as an ideologically based "threat" to them. Ironically, radical feminists believe that feminism is too closely identified with liberal feminism, a version of feminism that would be more acceptable to defacto feminists since their agendas and those of liberal feminists often coincide.

NOTES

1. As we will see in our subsequent discussions of this, the issue of women and work, the labor of single as well as married women in factories, is highly significant from the point of view of transformational politics. However, when discussing the ideology of patriarchy, the descriptive emphasis needs to be placed on the already established paradigm.

2. Judith Stacey (1982) examines the issues raised by "conservative pro-family feminists," and appears to be the first to use that expression.

3. There have been a number of comprehensive approaches to the different types of feminism. Rosemarie Tong's *Feminist Thought* is recommended, as well as Marianne Hirsch and Evelyn Fox Keller's *Conflicts in Feminism*. The latter is an attempt to bridge the distance among various expressions of feminism be emphasizing points of dialogue.

4. Patriarchy is "a system of male authority which oppresses women through its social, political and economic institutions. In any of the historical forms that patriarchal society takes, whether it is feudal, capitalist or socialist, a sex-gender system and a system of economic discrimination operate simultaneously. Patriarchy has power from men's greater access to, and mediation of, the resources and rewards of authority structures inside and outside the home" (Humm, 1990: 159).

5. This is made clear in the piece written by Carrie Chapman Catt in the *New York Times*, Feb. 15, 1914. There she goes to great pains as to insure readers that the suffrage movement was not about "free-love," or other radical notions, but only about the vote.

6. When the author was discussing the ideology surrounding Secretaries' Day at a large state university, several students reacted quite strongly to the suggestion of an ideology used to justify job segregation. They were quite adamant in their defense of their right to receive flowers on Secretaries Day. The phrase *raises not roses* seemed to offend some of them.

7. In particular, the *New York Times* ran a series of op-ed pieces debating the alleged disdain of feminists for the nursing profession. See, for example, "The Feminist Disdain for Nursing," Ellen D. Baer, the *New York Times* (op-ed page), March 11, 1991.

Chapter 4

De Facto Feminism and the Politics of Identity

Having examined the initial historical, institutional, structural, and ideological reasons why women do not identify themselves as feminists, even while accepting the goals of feminism, we are now in a better position to ask what the phenomenon of de facto feminism has to contribute toward feminist identity per se.

In the TV version of feminist identification the moment when an individual becomes a feminist is marked by changes in clothing, in one's style of hair, and hopefully as far as commercial interests are concerned, it is marked by something else--the initiation of a huge change in the brand names that one uses--everything from personal checks to cigarettes. This is, of course, a caricature of the actual state of affairs, but even in sophisticated discussions of feminist identification, it is still difficult to escape that discourse whereby feminism amounts to a myriad of changes in the things with which one surrounds oneself, and the behaviors that correspond to those changes.

What we will be stressing in this analysis is that behavioral changes, as well as the alterations in the accouterments of life, represent a second level of change, and that the primary change is an ontological one--that feminism involves a certain way of being. It is characterized by a changes in relationships and a recognition of a series of empirical conditions, the result of which is a transformational praxis informed by autonomy.

Autonomy in this sense is not a value that one receives from without; but rather it is the intentional content of a recognition on the part of de facto feminists of what it means to be a woman in a society that is marked by patriarchal ideology on the one hand, and capitalist social relations (characterized by extreme competition) on the other. It is to recognize, as Jane Mansbridge put it recently, "that a woman may be one man, or one paycheck away from welfare."[1]

In this depiction of de facto feminist identity it is no longer a matter of assigning a single meaning to identity, but of presenting as many sides of this intentional matrix as is relevant and possible. Transformational praxis, for this reason, while using the words "materialist," or, on occasion, "subjectivity," does so not as a final causal explanation, but as so many points of reference to what is essentially a process of self-generation through acting to change one's status. What this means is that identity, in this case de facto feminist identity, is not caused by material conditions, but neither is it caused by the acceptance from without of feminist identity. It is, instead, immanent to the individual woman and develops out of that praxis that recognizes the contradictory status of women in patriarchal capitalism. Like all praxis it represents an attempt to overcome a conflict in experience. Thus, when we describe this state of affairs as exhibiting autonomy, we are describing the fact that a specific woman recognizes this condition and has decided to act in terms of her own self-interest.

Self-interest and autonomy, however while they certainly can refer to an ideological perspective on the world, where one "looks out for oneself first," is not what we mean when we refer to self-interest and autonomy as ontological terms. The ontological meaning of these terms refers to the onset of a praxis designed to address the condition of women, which, as we have stressed, is not ideological, but existential. De facto feminism, then, can be thought of as a kind of existential imperative.

In order to underscore the nonideological character of de facto feminism it may be useful to examine some aspects of the work of economist Barbara Bergmann. One of the controversial claims of Bergmann's work is her discussion of women's need to work. It is her contention that the idea of the need to work is not empirically accurate in many cases, and it is instead, designed to facilitate acting against the ideological prohibition of doing so (for example, women *should be home with children*). Bergmann's argument and explanation of the "need to work" concept is a complex one that falls outside of our discussion here. The importance for us is Bergmann's point that the very act of taking a job outside the home for some middle-class married women was and remains "a stigmatized act" (Bergmann, 1986: 32).

It is an interesting debate, but what is more important in this context is our position that beneath the discourse on the need to work lies a prior existential awareness of women's condition in society, and, that it is this recognition that ultimately drives the process forward. Bergmann's analysis underscores a more general point--that the progression of this development is tangible and nonideological.

ECONOMIC EMERGENCE AS AN EXPRESSION OF TRANSFORMATIONAL POLITICS

Patriarchy and patriarchal attitudes were well established long before the nineteenth century and certainly were well entrenched in the early days of women's entrance into the nondomestic labor force. Therefore, the approval and emergence of women working outside the home for wages was a significant development in the history of women's liberation.

It did, however, cut both ways. On the one hand, the demands of industrial capitalism undercut the empirical basis of the ideology of the family, as can be seen in some of the writings of labor leaders from the period. The following quote from a labor leader of the day is useful not only because it captures the prevailing notion about women that existed in the AFL, but because the line of argument will be a familiar one to latter day feminists as well. For, it is illustrative of a view that one still hears on occasion:

The growing demand for female labor is not founded upon philanthropy, as those who encourage it would have sentimentalists believe; it does not spring from the milk of human kindness. It is an insidious assault upon the home; it is the knife of the assassin, aimed at the family circle--the divine injunction. Capital thrives not upon the peaceful, united contented family circle; rather are its palaces, pleasures and vices fostered and increased upon the disruption, ruin or abolition of the home, because with its decay and ever glaring privation manhood loses its dignity, its backbone, its aspirations. (Cott, 1979: 349)

Women's entrance into the economy opened up new ways of providing for themselves outside the traditional family model. In so doing, it also provided a new status that was missing in some of the more traditional forms of labor, such as domestic work. Already by 1905, economist Barbara Bergmann tells us, labor market segmentation by sex was a growing trend. Along with it, there was another trend: the increasing percentage of women in the labor force for longer periods of time. Bergmann makes the point in *The Economic Emergence of Women* that this corresponds with a rise in the value of women's labor time. Interestingly, it also corresponds with a decline in the number of childbirths.

As support for this first point, Bergmann highlights the growth in earnings for women workers between 1890 and 1984. Her statistics show a dramatic increase through the period. "The data indicate that women's real wages have more then quadrupled since 1890. The quantity of commodities a woman could buy with the earnings from an hour's work at a job has grown by 1.64 percent per year, on average, between 1890 and 1985" (Bergmann, 1986: 26, fig. 2-2). In addition, between 1870 and 1986, women as a percentage of the labor force grew from 16 percent to 44 percent. As she puts it: "Every decade after 1880 shows an increase in the percentage of the labor force that is female" (Bergmann, 1986: 20). Bergmann makes the case that the major structural changes we have seen are primarily the result of developing capitalism. It is her position that "the key to women's economic emergence is that women's time has risen in price until it has become too valuable to be spent entirely in the home" (Bergmann, 1986: 17).

Although we can see de facto feminism in the realm of economics, this is only after a prior event has taken place--the recognition of women's precarious economic status in a society gradually defined by the contingencies of first national, and then multinational, capitalism. It is all to easily overlooked that the development of capitalism during the period that Bergmann discusses brought with it enormous social dislocation and upheaval in the United States. Although many commentators are quick to point out the harshness of this same process going on in Central Europe and in Russia, we seem to fail to remember this aspect of American history. Yet, it was during this period in U.S. history, during the movement from national to multinational capitalism, that the radical changes in the structure of the family took place. Along with the extensive growth in urban populations and manufacturing came the development of new social relationships that represented something of a Faustian bargain with developing capitalism. There was an exchange of the protection and security provided by the extended family for the consumerist orientation and telos of the nuclear family. Within the context of these new social relationships the contingency of women's existence increased exponentially. It is then, in this context of new social relationships, brought on by emerging multinational capitalism, that a praxis developed that was intended to address the new contingency--de facto feminism. Thus, when conservatives express concern over the alleged demise of the family, wishing to return to earlier times and seeking to place the blame at the doorstep of feminism, they are engaging in abstraction of the worse sort.

Bergmann's work allows us to view this praxis from a societal level. Additional light can be shed on transformational politics by examining in some detail a specific instance of women's economic activity and praxis. The Johnson Controls Case affords us an excellent opportunity to do so. In the Johnson Controls Case, seemingly unfeminist women, simply performing their daily activities at a factory, came into contact with a new policy at Johnson Controls. Since 1982, Johnson Controls, the largest maker of batteries for cars, developed a policy intended not only to keep women from working in factory jobs that exposed them to lead, but also to prevent them from entering positions which might *possibly* lead to these higher paying positions. The promulgation of the policy generated an attempt on the part of these middle-aged factory workers to transform their experience into one that was more equitable. Women were being asked to give up these jobs or prove that they were not fertile. Even women who were beyond their reproductive years were compelled to demonstrate their inability to bear children. Many women in their child-bearing years were forced to choose sterilization rather than lose their income. No men were subjected to this policy, even though research demonstrated that sperm could be adversely affected by the battery lead.

It is important to note the context within which the new policy arose. Johnson Controls was not alone in drafting the policy, but was a part of a larger trend among chemical and other manufacturing corporations drafting so-called fetal protection policies not out of enlightened concern, but out of a fear of lawsuits. These were the same companies "whose histories suggest that they would welcome an excuse to exclude women" (Faludi, 1991: 437). The policies themselves were combined with a revamped ideology that included arguments concerning women's essential differences from men.

What is of interest here, however, is the sharp contrast that is to be drawn between the women of Johnson Controls and the typical image of feminism in many media portrayals. These were middle-aged, working-class women about whom little could be found that would distinguish them politically from the millions of other women who fit their demographic profile. The decision to act, to initiate a political praxis that eventually raised the consciousness of the feminist movement itself, even while promoting their own individual goals, has something to say about transformational praxis.

The highly visible institutional political and legal efforts on behalf of the women of Johnson Controls should not obscure the dynamics of the process of transformational praxis, which preceded and informed the legal strategy. It is precisely because the legal avenue of political conflict resolution is the predominant one in the United States, that it often appears to be the case that discontinuous, inchoate mountains of litigation seem apolitical, where in fact they have been part and parcel of an earlier relationship that we have characterized as transformational praxis, which itself rests on a relational ontology. The women of Johnson Controls initiated a transformational praxis not because they were informed from without, but because they engaged with their situation in the course of their daily lives.

The upshot is that when we focus on activity, such as empirical support for economic equality, we arrive at a much different conception of who is and who is not a feminist, and what is and is not political. By pursuing economic self-interest, the women of Johnson Controls were acting nonideologically. They already had an accurate picture of their self-interest. And, it is in the economic sphere that we find the most stark expression of women pursuing their own self-interest, even against the prevailing ideology. One of Bergmann's contributions is the delineation of just how effective women have been in asserting their political/economic interests even while undermining traditional ideology. Bergmann's depiction of the need to work underscores the central role of factual experience in women's successful dismantling of one ideology by formulating an equally compelling ideology based on the new factual experience--that of the *need to work* (Bergman, 1986). What this part of the analysis seems to imply is that de facto feminism elucidates the difference between feminism defined as ideology and feminism as praxis. We are able to discern that both the analysis and phenomenon of de facto feminism proceed on completely different tracks than does the ideology of feminism. It is easy to overlook the reality that informs de facto feminism and the question of identity that it presupposes by focusing solely on political attributes now extant.

FEMINIST IDENTITY AS RELATIONAL ONTOLOGY AND ENTITATIVE ONTOLOGY

Having stressed the point of view of transformational praxis whereby feminist identity is ontological as opposed to ideological, we should now turn our attention to a depiction of that ontology. In a word, it means that the ontology on which identity rests is to be understood as perigrinal as opposed to entitative.[2] When we refer to a relational ontology, we mean to emphasize the fact that it is perigrinal, or under way and in the process of becoming. Some brief historical context may serve to illustrate the distinction between these two differing visions of identity.

Entitative ontology is perhaps the one with which we are most familiar, and in fact what I want to suggest is not two opposing onto-logies, but ones which ideally are complementary. However, because the grounding of political discourse is either one or the other, for all practical purposes they remain oppositional. An entity is what it is in virtue of its sameness through time, and so we can speak of a person in a general way, in much the same way that we speak of other entities. Moreover, this individual has more or less set characteristics that distinguish him or her that we can appeal to when we interact socially. Within political theory, it is fair to say that entitative ontology is the bedrock on which social contract theory is developed.

Perigrinal ontology, however, is quite different and reflects those voices in the history of philosophy who have viewed change as the very essence of ontology. Heraclitus, of course, is the name that is most often associated with this idea, but there is a continuity of thought from Heraclitus through Eckhart, and that is very much a part of twentieth-century European philosophy.[3]

Relational ontology as perigrinal, however, does not only refer to change as the basic state of reality, but to the self as radically other than entities. While we can speak with confidence about the continuity of entities, this is precisely not the case with the self, for whom identity can never be fully fixed in the same way that of an entity is. This latter aspect of relational ontology has been reinforced by an additional perspective in philosophy--that of intentionality. Here, the idea is that the self is always in the process of becoming, and it merges with the notion that, since consciousness is always consciousness of something, the relations that we establish through intentionality (and which are referenced back), constitute the essence of the individual to the degree to which we can refer to an essence. There are then three distinguishing features of a relational ontology--change, self-transformation, and intentionality.

The latter two of these features, self-transformation and intentionality, have received considerable support over the years from the study of early childhood development. The recognition of the other that the child experiences prior to or simultaneous with his or her own recognition as other has already been well researched and documented. The same can be said of intentionality, which has been employed in generations of phenomenological research.

Clearly, the most controversial claim about relational ontology is the idea and extent to which change is the most accurate backdrop for discussions of identity. Initially, of course, one needs to address the issue of the degree of change. Even the most conservative thinkers would admit to some change in the self, but not to the degree that it constitutes the being of the self. However, if we are speaking about changes in identity, it would appear that the extent of change involved is quite substantial, and so the argument against relational ontology, whereby a degree of change is accommodated within an entitative construct, seems not to hold.

Because we are viewing the self in a nonentitative way, any examples we choose to illustrate relational ontology would necessarily involve history, either as applied to the person or to society (since we can only notice change after it has occurred). The first illustration is Judith Butler's account of psychic mimesis, which she uses to explicate some features of sexual identity.

A Freudian term, psychic mimesis refers to the process whereby the self retains the presence of the other through taking on his or her ways of being. Butler maintains that it is this, and not the playing out of an inherent human nature, that helps to account for the diversity of human sexuality. Psychic mimesis, however, is incompatible with an entitative view of ontology. If one were to explain the diversity of human sexuality by way of an entatative ontology, one would probably need to go in a different direction, since the self, which takes on these new ways of being, is a real self, and it is not an artificially grafted-on construct. On the contrary, it becomes a part of the intentional structure.

This presentation of this aspect of relational ontology is at odds, quite obviously, with a conservative view of the world and the self. Moreover, as we move to the level of society in political discourse, it is not unusual for specific groups to come into conflict over competing understandings of what the basic structure of human reality is and how that is to be organized politically. As Gelb and Palley noted (1978), our politics is never sharper then when we move from changes that accommodate existing roles to those that involve wholesale role change itself.

In some of his early works, Sartre noted the propensity of the other to continually turn one into a thing, or to transform the for-itself into an in-itself. In fact, the self engages in this process as well, seeking always to find that solidity that is the hallmark of a thing. While Sartre later refined this perspective, dropping some aspects of it in favor of others, it continues to provide an excellent point of origin for a discussion of the politics of identity. For, the refusal to recognize the developmental nature of ontology and transformation takes place through the continual appeal to and buttressing of the entitative model of the self, and consequently, of identity.

We can see the politics of this a bit more clearly in the case of de facto feminist identity where much of the politics has centered on the disapproval against the women's movement away from the traditional expressions of identity. The historical analysis presented earlier in this book has established the fact that the ideology of patriarchy has continually invoked the past model as the pattern that necessarily should be followed. To a certain extent then, the de facto feminist decision to bracket out the label feminist involves a recognition that one can never win the debate with conservatives using a conservative ontology. When de facto feminists engage in practical activity that establishes at every moment the relevance of a relational ontology, they accomplish much more. They establish their autonomy in praxis, of course, but they also erode, by virtue of their acting, the existential basis for other ontological claims--those that would limit their freedom of action. Thus, de facto feminism established a transformation in the debate over identity, in this case feminist identity, by fiat. It is worth considering just how it is that de facto feminists bring this about. Here, we need to establish the relationship of de facto feminists to the wider, social movement of feminism in order to fully explicate how this fiat takes place.

The existence of an organizational structure was an important aspect of the transformational praxis we saw in Johnson Controls. The decision of the women of Johnson Controls was an autonomous one. However, once these women decided to act, the National Organization for Women (NOW) became the means by which a reciprocal relationship developed between individual praxis and the wider social movement. The offer of legal and financial resources by NOW complemented the earlier individual action of the women involved, while on the other hand, the wider community of women, as well as the organization itself, gained a deeper understanding of the specific forms that the movement of feminism needed to address, in this case the specific needs of working-class women. We can say then, that relational ontology gave way to a reciprocal process of consciousness-raising whereby the individual actors were enabled to see the larger, historical meaning of their actions, while members of the movement were made aware of the distinct particularities--the specifics--of transformational praxis. This reciprocal consciousness-raising, however, follows from the action and the capacity of the women involved to establish a series of relationships.

If we look further at the example of Johnson Controls we can see that the conflict between the women of Johnson Controls and management was over the issue of relational ontology, and specifically over the perigrinal and entitative distinction. The policy that was initiated by Johnson Controls reflected a cultural assessment, as well as an entitative one--that there is an essential difference between men and women, and that men and women are to be defined in an entitative way. Casting the discussion in terms of entitative ontology, instead of merely saying that the policy reflected an essentialist view of women and men, allows the actual politics at work to be seen more clearly. For, politics can often appear benign when its invokes the language of essentialism. It is quite another matter, however, when we insist on the entitative distinction, for then we see that the real issue is the attempt to view individuals as things and to forsake the ethical requirements of considering their humanity.

In Johnson Controls, where "safety" was used as the basis for discrimination, the politics was hidden under the pretext of concern over environmental health. However, it took place against the backdrop of a widespread effort to limit the developmental choices of working women. The effort against Johnson Controls was initiated by women who had little, if any, exposure to feminist organizing efforts. Viewed from a legal perspective, the situation appears quite the reverse, as a legal action by definition does not begin until after a claim has been filed, which in the case of Johnson Controls, was well after the factual initiation of political praxis.

One additional aspect of Johnson Controls that is interesting from the point of view of relational ontology, and from the point of view of de facto feminism and the question of identity, is the way in which the ideology that surrounds feminist identity was bracketed in favor of a more specific discussion of the actual issues at work in de facto feminist praxis--issues such as equity, child-care responsibility, and any number of politically grounded policies. It represents first, a recognition of the politics that feminism elicits--that the very word "feminist" or "feminism" generates the negative media portrayals of the past and the departure from the entitative landscape of political discourse. Second, their bracketing of ideology is an attempt to override these negative images by choosing to start a discussion beyond the threshold of the ideology of feminist identity.

It seems that this bracketing of the term is intended as a political strategy designed to bypass the ideology surrounding feminist identity in order to initiate a substantive discussion of the social justice that underlie a specific issue such as equality, child care, or reproductive rights.

One final aspect of the relationship between ontology and the politics of identity has to do with the issue of expectations. It has become, of course, something of a mainstay in the social sciences that rising expectations are politically volatile. What we see in the case of de facto feminism is that changes in one's place in society conform not only to one's expectations but to a certain ontological location as well. Reproductive rights, for example, seem to imply the expectation that one's ontological status, and hence identity as well, is in one's own hands.

This ontological feature of expectations is a component of a more general gestalt politics, wherein other expectations are related so that changes in some will influence others. Paula Kamen, in her analysis of young women and feminism, notes that expectations inform their understanding of feminism, and consequently, of the kind of world they will live in. It is an expectational gestalt where the removal of these expectations seems absurd. Kamen quotes one young women to make the point that expectations of feminism have come to be taken for granted to such an extent that: "It [feminism] is such a basic part of culture that everyone takes it for granted" (Kamen, 1991: 38).

What is unique about the relational ontology that is contained in the philosophy of praxis is that it addresses the age-old problem of the individual and the community in such a way that the emphasis is placed on the relationship--where political activity is not something "out there," but is something immanent to the individual's existence. In discussing identity, we saw that this approach reformulates agency so that individual action, of the kind we saw in Johnson Controls, is grounded in the individual's capacity to establish a relationship--something decidedly nonentitative.

The decision made by women to view discriminatory working conditions, as in the case of Johnson Controls, as something more than just their own personal problem placed them in a relationship to the wider social movement that is reciprocally empowering because of its linkages to both previous and continuing praxes. The very same socialization process that initially can be limiting can also raise expectations and awareness of historical issues (Ferree and Hess, 1985; Cott, 1987).

One consequence of this is that the decision to act, as the women of Johnson Controls did, is also a decision to locate one's self in a wider field of resources and to view one's situation within a feminist context, or to establish a feminist world view. This would seem to imply that at the level of individual praxis, and on the basis of relational ontology, disparate choices are internally related such that they bring one into a relationship to the unorganized and organized feminist movement, both historically and in the present as a current and continuing political actor.

NOTES

1. Comments delivered during a discussion of the significance of 1996 election results and covered by C-Span.

2. Reiner Schurmann (1978) makes the distinction between perigrinal and entitative ontology initially in his work on Meister Eckhart. His notes in that work contain a number of interesting references to the relationship between Eckhart and Hegel. The work itself is an important bridge between early philosophies of change and those of more modern vintage. At the center of these philosophies is the ontology by which and through which their concepts are formed, an excellent representative of which is Schurmann's account of Eckhart.

3. Here I would also cite Robert Jay Lifton's influential work on the protean self. The initial article appeared in a collection entitled *The Existential Mind*. A later treatment is his book by the same title. It is interesting to note that his later work was criticized for having presented the human capacity for continuous radical change as something good.

Chapter 5

De Facto Feminism and the Feminist Movement

This chapter will present the evidence that the existence and the contribution of de facto feminists becomes obvious during certain political moments within the history of the feminist movement. One of these was the protest surrounding the 1989 Webster Decision. In order to fully understand Webster and its relationship to de facto feminism it may be useful to say a word about several biases that serve to exclude de facto feminism from many political analyses.

For quite some time some feminist scholars have noted a bias in political science's understanding of women and political participation. Briefly put, the problem is that it has historically been the case that a great deal of women's political activity was extra-legislative and involved efforts far removed from the usual categories of political analysis--voting behavior, congressional lobbying, and presidential politics. This bias defined political activity along the categories just mentioned, and unless one formally engaged in them, then one was simply acting outside of the political sphere (Fowkes, 1989). Later scholarship, especially movement scholarship, began to raise questions about these approaches, especially in the light of the clearly political nature of the extra legislative protests that went on during the 1960s and 1970s, and which, to a lesser extent have continued into the present. Grudgingly, political science has begun to accept the notion of a broad understanding of political participation. However, often when presenting ideas that reflect a more expansive notion of political participation (which, as I will discuss, is implied in a praxis approach), one is made aware of some discomfort on the part of mainstream political science. The discomfort comes across in statements by some political scientists that there is a need to reestablish the old boundaries that reflect the traditional formula whereby the political is equated with the public sphere and the non-political is equated with the private sphere. However, simple analysis of the fact that the political acts from which republics are founded (as witnessed in Eastern Europe and the States of the former Soviet Union) explicitly indicate a wider conception of politics and not the formal one. Additionally, many so-called private issues have become the basis of changes in voting behavior, which would confound the conviction of the absolute separation of political activity from other compartments of social life. What is of particular concern for this analysis is the idea that by accepting narrow conceptions of what it means to be politically active and by insisting upon a strict separation of economics from politics, praxis as a vehicle for identifying the political activity of de facto feminists is ruled out. It is this that constitutes the essence of the first bias in political science--that praxis is missing as a category of analysis. This work then, can be seen as an effort to reestablish praxis as the basis of political activity, and the concept of de facto feminism put forth here is among other things, the means for the introduction of praxis. By looking at political activity through praxis, additional avenues of political debate emerge and new questions arise that may previously have been ignored or considered outside the "political."

One example of this is the effort of feminists to bring about national child care. Prior to the feminist-initiated debate over the issue, child care was thought to be a personal issue and was considered to be unrelated to the area of public policy and politics. Despite this, feminists have succeeded in bringing this issue into the forefront of political debate. Praxis is activity-centered, and because of this it places the focus on the actions of members in a community. One aspect of this is that using praxis for the analysis of social movements has the effect of expanding "the political." A number of theorists have used this approach to study women (Bookman and Morgan, 1988: Fowkes, 1989), and they specifically make the point that many aspects of women and politics are excluded from consideration simply because they take place outside of the prescribed areas and venues usually considered "political." Their argument is that community organizing by women on issues ranging from transportation to resource allocation later becomes the basis of political praxis and allows us to locate the mechanism by which transformation takes place. It is also their position that many assessments of working-class women's political action specifically suffers from a bias that stresses institutional approaches (legislation, office holding, etc). The result, they say, is that there is far less treatment within the literature on social movements of women's activities, as working women's political activity takes place in community settings at the grassroots level (Bookman and Morgan, 1988). In their view this has led to the rise in theories that narrowly constitute the political (Bookman and Morgan, 1988; 3). Bookman and Morgan's work stresses not only the need for an expansive notion of "the political," but also places the emphasis on "objective" or "material" political action. However, as theorists of *cognitive praxis* have underscored, since praxis seeks to convey the unity between the "subjective" and the "objective," constituting a third form of social ontology, the initiation of a praxis of freedom intended to overcome a conflict in experience does not imply that the conflict is primarily a material one.

An additional bias in political science has to do with epistemology. Because praxis is an account of political transformation from the ground up, it seeks to avoid an epistemological bias that exists within some approaches to social movements, namely focusing on leadership and the formal structures that link a movement to other movements. An alternative feminist theory of leadership, one based on praxis and that follows the contributions of this study, is presented in the concluding chapter of this book.

What makes this bias particularly insidious is that its epistemology tends to reinforce itself through theory. Because it focuses on the leaders of a movement, and then works down to the grassroots level, it naturally focuses also on the *beliefs* and *ideas* of the movement's leadership. The upshot is that epistemological problem whereby the *consciousness* of leaders is privileged over the *activity* of members.

There are some serious consequences to this epistemological perspective. First, judgments about a movement's success or growth can be negatively predetermined by the degree to which members receive the belief systems of leaders. With this account it would seem to follow that a successful movement is one where all the members have a shared belief system and a shared conception of self-identity. Finally, these belief systems and preconceptions of identity in turn, may be used to measure and gauge the success of a social movement. One political consequence of this, of course, is that a large number of its members are left out of consideration. In a political environment where interest-group competition is the norm, the failure to be perceived as having sufficient "numbers," or members who identify with a movement, can often mean political ostracism. There are, however, additional consequences that are not just political.

Considering the feminist movement from the epistemological model outlined above would mean that the feminist movement is successful to the degree to which women express a preference for a core set of ideas and beliefs. However, the very diversity of women as well as the uneven exposure to social change that characterizes regional differences in the United States, to say nothing of race and class, seems to call into question the usefulness of this epistemology. The privileging of consciousness implies a greater role for the use of *rhetoric* by leaders. In this model, movement change happens when leaders successfully use rhetoric to mobilize women to political action. However, as the examples outlined in this book illustrate, this is a rather incomplete account of how change comes about or has come about in the feminist movement. Instead, the feminist movement seems to demonstrate a reciprocal process whereby member actions, often in areas far removed from the leader's purview, *raise the consciousness of leaders*. Earlier, I cited the example of the women of Johnson Controls to make the point that the specificity that develops out of women's praxis is an important means by which theory is informed by praxis, thus making theory nonabstract.

This epistemological bias presents problems because it can be used strategically as the basis to argue against considering the claims made by those who advocate the cause of a social movement. This is especially the case if it can be shown that most of the likely members of a group do not agree with a set of beliefs, or the expression of a specific position on a survey questionnaire. Opponents of a social movement can argue that it follows that the leadership is out of touch with the "mainstream" of the likely members of a movement, claims can be delegitimized; and since a delegitimized movement is not likely to generate mobilized support, it can be ignored with very little in the way of political consequences. With mundane regularity the Right Wing often employs this tactic against African-American civil rights groups through the use of survey questionnaires designed to delegitimize organizational leadership. However, it is also used in the case of the feminist movement.

The context of American politics exacerbates the problems that stem from this epistemological bias. The emphasis that contemporary media coverage of politics places on a spectacle reinforces the tendency, already quite prevalent, to overvalue the contributions of spokespeople and leaders even while devaluing, or outright dismissing, the contributions made by the larger community.

Rather than viewing leaders as expressions of the inner workings and striving of a community, this bias essentially "abstracts out" the leaders and views them as of greater importance and as the fulcrum of change. If we look at the feminist movement, for example, we can see that this has often meant an overemphasis upon sensational media events and personalities, over and against the less sensational, but politically more important work of education, and progressive everyday praxis. However, this epistemology also creates problems for theories of feminism. Here, the problem is not that of omitting its participants, but consists in holding up theory as an undertaking outside of and separate from history. Consequently, theory is seen as possessing a timeless, ahistorical truth about the nature of social movements. Or, theory, in another version of the same problem (abstracted and separated from history), is viewed as human activity that is deficient and unreliable because of its separation from history. In both cases what is ignored is the fact that theory is human historical activity unthinkable as anything other than an effort to understand and make choices in a social world. In summary then, we can say that both of the instances of epistemological bias that we have considered result in the same problem--an abstract account of social movements.

PRAXIS AS AN ONTOLOGY OF SOCIAL MOVEMENTS

Carol Gould (1988) notes that all social theories include an ontology by which they explain the nature of social reality. The Western political tradition, as postmodernists have often noted, has emphasized ontology in terms of binary oppositions: realism and nominalism; idealist and materialist; and subjective and objective.

What a praxis approach has to offer to the question of the ontology of social movements, however, is an alternative approach to social reality; one that escapes the duality of the traditional ones while being grounded in human experience and avoiding abstraction. Theorists of praxis maintain that an accurate accounting of the ontology of social reality, of how social movements come about as well as how they are constructed, represents the first step toward an efficacious rendering of the relationships between the individual and the community. So, it represents a pivotal step in the political theory of social movements.

Gould does not make use of this tradition of ontology, but instead she turns to Marx's ontology of materialist dialectics. Gould is primarily interested in clearing a space for a theory of democracy that accounts for *both* the individual and the community, which she contends, in her early work, is to be found in Marx's *Grundrisse*. It is not necessary for her to describe *how* it is that the individual and the community are of equal value and depth. Gould maintains that in Marx's account, such a unity is accomplished. The philosophical tradition of praxis, that as I noted in Chapter Four, has deep roots in Western thought, accounts for the how and the why of such an equality, and it does so in such a way that it provides for a nonelite (and, often cultural) account of social change as well. First, it may be useful at this point to touch on the idea of political transformation in some of the traditional non-praxis approaches.

Approaches to the nexus between collective action and the individual have been the source of a considerable amount of debate within the field. On the one hand, there is an open revolt against early social psychology and its formulation of collective action, which have been viewed as reductionist and antidemocratic. On the other hand, the rational choice approach, with its own underlying assumptions of the maximization of personal benefits and the reduction of costs, has also come under attack in the literature.

The difficulty seems to lie in the complexity that attends the relationship between individual action and the social movement. It appears to be because of the free and necessarily contingent nature of this relationship that models of social action that stress the goals of leaders do not appear to present an accurate account of social movements, since they generally ignore the direct effects of grassroots activity, which is where we have located de facto feminism. In contrast to a teleological account de facto feminism stresses a gestalt political reality in which features of the totality of the movement interact with, and are internally related to the totality in such a way that changes in the features influence the totality.[1] Thus, not only is theory, a form of political activity, but so are many of the other social activities that de facto feminists engage in. All of these influence the totality so that, at the level of the social movement, relational ontology is an appropriate term for describing the nexus between de facto feminists and the feminist movement.

De facto feminism belongs to a movement outside the normal avenues of political discourse, and, for this reason, has not been considered in American politics. Viewed from the point of view of the study of social movements, de facto feminism points beyond itself and raises those questions we considered earlier about the study of the nature of social movements. On this score, it is important to recall some comments made by Costain in her discussion of social movements: "Social movements raise serious questions outside normal government channels, often concerning subjects which are not being treated as topics of political concern" (Costain, 1990: 169). Yet, how could this be the case unless those who are raising the concern, which as we saw in Johnson Controls involves women who are not necessarily feminists, are themselves internally related to the social movement in some way?

The position we have been taking in the development of the concept of de facto feminism is that de facto feminism is not the same as the organized form of feminism, but yet it constitutes a major base of support for feminism even while being largely unacknowledged. Special attention should, it seems, also be paid to Costain's position that "Movements encompass both organized groups and unorganized, and usually indeterminate, numbers of followers" (Costain, 1990: 169).

This latter point is underscored by the 1992 protests over the Webster Decision. It accomplishes by way of historical example what we have already outlined by our discussion of theory--the way in which feminist praxis out paces, and is prior to, but not separate from, theory.

Susan Faludi, writing about the Webster Decision, notes:

The US Supreme Court's 1989 Webster decision, that upheld state restrictions on abortion, was the culmination of years of backlash against Roe vs. Wade. This was done by hundreds of legislative maneuvers that led to prohibitive rules and consent notifications in more than 30 states. . . . the final straw came in 1991 when the US Supreme Court allowed the government to prohibit federally funded clinics from even speaking about abortion when counseling pregnant women. (Faludi, 1991: 420)

The April 1992 response to the Webster Decision was one of the largest women's rights demonstrations in U.S. history. What is extraordinary about the Webster demonstration, however, is not the scope of the response but the theoretical circumstances under which it occurred, and what this has to say about theories of social change. It took place during a period of time that by all accounts was perceived to be one of women's lack of engagement in American politics. Susan Faludi's work, for example, chronicles the era as replete with ideologically driven references to a supposed widespread belief in a newly emergent conservatism by American women, who were victims of backlash driven studies of ticking biological clocks that women could ignore only at their peril (Faludi, 1991: 421).

Because of this widespread perception of a conservative mood among women, the Webster demonstration and the mobilization leading up to it afford us an example of a praxis account of social movements against the backdrop of a failure to account for it by means of some survey analyses. One reason for this, as Donahue notes, is that the vast majority of movement scholarship ignored a substantive portion of the feminist movement (Donahue, 1996: 62). But more important perhaps is the question of why it was ignored.

The organizational efforts for the march faced an audience that was not only well versed in the issues confronting feminism in the 1990s, but one that had already expanded the day-to-day meaning of feminism itself. Thus, to a certain extent, the limitations involved in a nonpraxis approach to feminist identity are highlighted by the response to the Webster demonstration, which surprised even its organizers. In order to account for the overwhelming response of women to the demonstration one would have to seek an explanation that accounts for those who are self-identified feminists, as well as those who routinely engage in politics. However, in order to do so one needs just that wider view of politics and an expanded view of feminism, which we have stressed by the introduction of de facto feminism.

One might question the historical status of de facto feminism during periods of dormancy, which may eventually take on the explicitly political character we see in episodes like Webster. The question can be put--just how is it that one might account for such episodes, given years, or even decades of formal and explicit political inactivity. One answer to this is that while de facto feminism is a historically related to a praxis designed to overcome a problem in experience and social life, it is possible to discern the presence of de facto feminism if one approaches the study of social phenomena from an ontology of relations. For example, there have been numerous studies of women and their positions on any number of issues. Often, however, these questionnaires are separated from theory, and the answers themselves are reduced by the media into factoids, manipulable political grist for the next campaign cycle. An alternative is to view the connections between respondents and to inquire into the social conditions and relations that are implied by their answers.

A number of years ago, the *New York Times* did a major survey in which it asked the attitudes of women toward a number of social issues. They were specifically asked their perspective on a variety of questions dealing with aspects of feminism. As one might expect, the evidence on this issue seems to support the idea that younger women, because they are beneficiaries of the efforts of women who came before them, are more accepting of feminist ideas and even the label itself. This seems to underscore the issue of political expectations and feminism since, as Paula Kamen notes, it is usually the case that younger women view feminism as a normal or ordinary feature of social life. On the contrary, for older women, it was anything but ordinary. A separate issue is, of course, the relationship of older women's praxis to the unorganized feminist movement. However, the point that needs to be made is that although there may be important generational differences, the emphasis on attitude differences should not cause us to overlook a positive assessment of feminism that may be present in the praxis of older women.

It seems to underscore that as more women in younger generations become economically independent and/or aware of the need for independence (and are less resident in the "traditional" private sphere), support for a strong women's movement increases. Also, even older women, more likely to have grown up in the "private sphere," are increasingly advocating a strong women's movement as more of them face the challenges of becoming wage earners to support their family. Based on a notion of praxis, then, the group of women "doing feminist things" far surpasses women who consider themselves feminists and thus supports the notion of the existence of a large number of de facto feminists. Yet, the survey was conducted during the height of the antifeminist years (generally speaking, the 1980s), and so we would have expected to see that these women would be less interested in feminism, especially among young women! The news was full of reports, well chronicled by Susan Faludi's book *Backlash* (1991), of a growing lack of interest in feminism and a growing trend that viewed feminism as irrelevant.

It also tells us something else, however--that the broad support for feminism shows the extent to which the goals of feminism are separable from the label "feminist." This survey and others like it contradicted the many commentaries that were prevalent and should have raised alarms of the sort Faludi describes. A closer examination of polling indicates, as Ferree and Hess note, that "Attitudes toward the feminist movement itself have become steadily more positive: from 40 percent of women in favor of most efforts to strengthen and change women's status in society in 1970 to 64 percent in 1980, and 77 percent in 1990. Ferree and Hess cite Roper to make their point and conclude by stating that many media outlets, "Rather than highlighting the positive numbers," tended to "draw attention to nonfeminist responses" (Ferree and Hess, 1985: 88-89). At this juncture it may be useful to establish one of the connections that the survey question seems to reveal--that of de facto feminists and patriarchy at the level of the social movement.

PATRIARCHY AND DE FACTO FEMINISM

One of the elements of the problem of modern feminism with regard to support for feminist goals is the extent to which women recognize their self-interest in the face of an ideology that works at cross-purposes with it. It is a context we just defined--where women have said, on the one hand that there is a need for a strong feminist movement, and on the other that they themselves are not feminists. This raises the issue of patriarchy--the ideology of male sexual hierarchy, which contends that, among other things, women's self-interest is best served by the denial of equality with men and a voluntary or coerced ceding of personal freedom. Becoming aware of and actively supporting one's own self-interest against the backdrop of a strong countervailing ideology is, after all, anything but a forgone conclusion.

One explanation for women's ability to discern their self-interests despite the presence of an alternative ideology (liberalism) is provided by Zillah Eisenstein. It is an argument that also supports the view presented here about *de facto* feminist *praxis* as activity that runs counter to the ideology of patriarchy, even while not directly addressing the issue of patriarchy as an ideology. As noted earlier, Zillah Eisenstein makes this exact point in arguing that "women's equality of opportunity (liberalism) continues to undermine the patriarchal privilege on which the liberal state is based, even though many of these feminists (liberal feminists) do not fully recognize the radical feminist content of their demands" (Z. Eisenstein, 1981: 231).

The dominant ideology is, of course, liberalism. It establishes, in Eisenstein's view, the rules of the game in such a way that de facto feminism enjoys a distinct advantage over patriarchy in making its case in American politics because patriarchal ideology is at odds with the equal opportunity upon which liberal rhetoric is based.

Eisenstein makes the additional point that "whereas the feminist demands of Wollenstonecraft, Mill, Taylor, and Stanton stood as radically liberal in their day, they are now part of the established ideology of the state" (Z. Eisenstein, 1981: 230). This point has to do with the importance of the conflict between patriarchy and liberal ideology. It also underscores the latter's reinforcement of the position of de facto feminists, and reciprocally, their contribution towards it.

With regard to patriarchy, equality has radical potential for both women and society, a position expressed by Eisenstein in both *The Radical Future of Liberal Feminism* and *Woman's Body and the Law*. We can see this radical element if we consider what would become of the social construction of gender if women were truly equal with men. In other words, complete equality with men implies, in effect, the elucidation and erosion of patriarchy.

Eisenstein's critique of liberal feminism is that it is a particular interpretation of feminism and the one which was the most accommodating to the established economic formation. The fact that its ascendancy was at the expense of other interpretations of feminism is important and should be noted. Her position, however, offers an explanation of the paradox of feminism. Her analysis takes the position that liberal feminism is the least threatening to modern capitalism and, as such, receives preferential treatment. Other versions, labeled "feminist," are given negative connotations by electronic and print media and are, predictably, rejected by public opinion. In a word, feminism receives negative spin.

Another of Eisenstein's contributions is the insight that the liberal notion of equality of opportunity is in direct opposition to the patriarchal notion of sexual hierarchy. Eisenstein critiques the idea that reality is composed only of ideas, or that alienation is basically an ideological problem (Z. Eisenstein, 1981). This is an important point, and it is one that seems to apply to a number of cultural analyses of the problems addressed by feminism. The difficulty is that in some instances cultural analyses go so far as to ahistorically argue that women's culture is responsible for the social changes ushered in by what was historically a political and economic struggle on the part of women. In our analysis, considerable attention has been paid to the importance of economics over ideology for de facto feminists. The position that it is in the economic sphere where inequality shows up most dramatically is supported by other survey questions posed to women. When asked what the most important problem that women face today, out of an extensive list including such high-profile issues as abortion, child care, and self-esteem, respondents chose "equal pay" as most important and, in general, preferred issues suggestive of economics over cultural or psycho-social concerns (*New York Times*, 1989). It is noteworthy that in the 1996 presidential campaign these same economic issues figured prominently on the list of women's concerns.

What is interesting about this result is the fact that equal pay, a political demand, receives so little attention in the media. To be sure, feminist organizations have had equality of pay as part of their platform for some time (Hartmann, 1989: 54). This would seem to support Bergmann's analysis, quoted earlier, regarding the pivotal role of economics in women's liberation, and finally, it highlights the need for an assessment of feminist identity that has examined women and political economy as part of its analysis. Instead, many analyses focus almost exclusively on cultural aspects of women in society, and if political economy is mentioned at all, it is usually the nightly news version, where women and political economy is reduced to dismissive, off-the-cuff remarks, such as: "Women continue to receive less on the dollar than do men."

Within economics, however, the equal pay issue is important for this analysis because it is directly related to Eisenstein's point concerning liberalism, here expressed as belief in equality of opportunity. In other words, equal pay as a goal "forces" the liberal notion of equality of opportunity both for individual women and for society in general into revealing a contradiction, which, as Eisenstein notes, is anything but mere liberalism when it is applied to women. But, how does the issue of equality of opportunity and the question of equal pay fit within the context of women's role in the traditional family and outside of the economy per se? We will consider one such attempt to raise equality of opportunity within the traditional context of the family: the Wages for Housework Movement of the 1970s.

Domestic work and the raising of children, a pathway that adheres to the traditional patriarchal scenario, does not allow for the discussion of equality of opportunity in the liberal democratic state because of its insistence upon separate spheres (public versus private). Instead, equality of opportunity requires women to be *outside* of the traditional role and *inside* the economic "public sphere." In fact, as already noted, women who remain in the traditional role often feel threatened as the ideological and economic underpinnings of their lifestyles are challenged and as equality of opportunity itself is seen as destructive of and detrimental to family values and family life. The concept of equality of opportunity within the context of the traditional family--where the husband works and the wife raises children and runs the household--received consider-able attention from Marxist/socialist feminists during the mid and late 1970s.[2] Marxist feminists argue that work in the home must be consid-ered as "work" necessary for the economy and, therefore, should be compensated. One expression of this was the movement called the "Wages for Housework Movement," which was an attempt to establish housework as productive labor in the Marxist sense of the term. However, it was never able to penetrate through the layers of ideology that proclaimed, at the time, that housework is a "labor of love."[3] Recently, many feminist economists have given estimates of the GNP that recognize and place a monetary value on women's work in the home.

Another social phenomenon that indicates broad support for the role of economics in the women's movement is the role in the military. Although a complete discussion of this topic is beyond the scope of our analysis, it needs to be considered here because of the weight it lends to the importance of praxis and economics. While it appears to be the case that women in the military represent simply a lifestyle issue, that assessment is an abstraction. By far the most universal reason for women entering the military is the economic benefits such membership provides, whether perceived in short-term goals, such as the paycheck itself, or longer-term goals, such as education.

The economic option for women that is implicit in their entrance into the military has of itself eliminated, almost unnoticed, one of the major arguments put forth to quell the (second wave) ERA movement. This important effort was accomplished not by consciousness-raising, but at the existential level by the daily activities of working-class women. It is important to recall the history of this event in order to fully appreciate the magnitude of the social change they wrought. At that time, the nonviability of the idea of women serving in quasi-combat roles was seen as justification to support the general distinction between men and women (for example sameness and difference) regarding human capability and equality and helped lead to the rejection of the ERA. Historically, one of the most powerful arguments used to maintain the sexual hierarchy has been that women are the weaker sex and need men for their defense, and that women should not serve in the military. Recently, the presence of women in the military had, in a de facto sense, made this entire line of reasoning obsolete. The focus of the debate has now shifted and is concerned with how much power women will exercise within the institutional structure of the military and the role of the state in increasing women's equality. On this issue, the fact of women serving in large numbers and at relatively high levels has simply overwhelmed patriarchal ideology. The reality of women's situation in the military was dramatized in the Persian Gulf crisis, when the media put forth the question of what happens when both parents are "over there." In fact (and almost inconceivably), the ensuing debate did *not* focus exclusively on the woman--the parenting role and responsibility of men were also examined, a situation almost impossible to imagine just a decade ago.

What cannot be disputed, it seems, is that to the extent that the military was and continues to be a major patriarchal institution, the actuality of women's entrance and performance in new military roles, its facticity, undermines the existence of patriarchy. This can be seen quite clearly by the explosion of sexual harassment claims in all branches of the military. It underscores just how entrenched and real patriarchy is, but it also highlights the fact that women are acting as significant agents of change in exactly those areas where patriarchy is most deeply entrenched. Seen in this way, the number of claims is an indication of just how successful women have been, for otherwise we would not hear of these claims--they would go unreported. These women are *agents* of considerable political and social change, especially so when seen from the point of view of praxis and political economy.

As has often enough been pointed out, women's entrance into nontraditional roles was accepted where the interests of society dictated an actual need for that accommodation. The famous example that comes to mind is that of "Rosie the Riveter" of World War II fame. What differentiates the current situation is that it is not a reflection of an *extraordinary* circumstance after which things will revert back to "normal," but, rather, an extension of a more *general* trend in American society as a whole. The economic emergence of women permeates all institutions of society, including the military. It is hard to imagine a scenario now where women are told to go back home.[4] The point that needs to be stressed however, is that based on the evidence we've examined so far, de facto feminism can be provisionally understood as individual women making choices that create greater freedom for women generally. Because of this, they belong to the general class of women who are "feminists" (i.e., based on their support for feminist goals), and what differentiates them from other members of this group is the fact that they may or may not identify themselves explicitly as feminists.

However, in order for this analysis not to fall victim to an ideological bias regarding what feminism is and is not, it is necessary that it arise out of the actions of women themselves, or remain phenomenological. These actions, through time, have shown themselves to involve a commitment to freedom of action. Therefore, an account of de facto feminism and its relationship to the feminist movement must start from this premise.

This premise has been a constant since the birth of the feminist movement, although its precise form has changed. Today, based on analyses presented earlier as well as the example of women in the military, the form of feminism centers around economic issues. In fact, what makes this phenomenon of change regarding women so significant is that it has occurred almost unnoticed. The importance of actual praxis over ideology, the latter of which, paradoxically, seems to be the usual basis for discussing identity, is further underscored by social phenomena that lie beyond the scope of this analysis, but which should perhaps be mentioned since they also have something to say about the relationship between de facto feminism and the feminist movement. When antifeminist women argue the case against feminism, their ideological arguments are refuted even as they speak by their own performance, which, in fact, presupposes feminist praxis.

Given the degree of change brought on by de facto feminist activity, how is it that such monumental change occurred without much acknowledgment? Does this reflect a societal bias that bypasses events having to do with women? Or is it simply the result of de facto feminism's tendency to maintain the existing ideology intact even as it makes that ideology irrelevant because it has been outpaced by the praxis of de facto feminism? With regard to de facto feminism, patriarchal ideology increasingly has come to resemble a seaside structure that continues to stand, but on the most precarious of stilts, its foundation long since eroded by the tide.

WOMEN AND HIGHER EDUCATION

The final area we want to touch on regarding the relationship between de facto feminist activity and feminism as a social movement is education. Radical changes in women's lives have been expressed not only in the institutions mentioned above (the economy, the political sphere, the military), but in higher education as well. The explosive growth of women in higher education has ushered in additional dimensions to the debate and has exacerbated the issue of equality of opportunity.

As women's access to education has grown over the past century, the tension between modernity and traditional roles has created areas of friction between men and women, with ideological attacks upon women drawn from traditional patriarchal antiwoman themes: irrationality, unpredictability, and general weakness.[5] Yet, as the labor force becomes increasingly driven by technological expertise, and as that expertise is accessed by women, the requirements of capitalism will continue to dictate that patriarchal ideology accommodate these new changes, or that social relationships support the overall economic context.

A paradigm for this was already witnessed during the 1980s when the American economy began to show the effects of the transition from heavy industry toward a service economy. Women came to comprise a large proportion of that employment area as American capitalism saw at once the value of a cheap, well-trained labor force.[6]

A subtext for this development has been the growth, albeit slow, of numbers of women in the natural sciences. While certain sciences, such as biology, have traditionally been open to women, others, such as physics, because of factors related to the socialization process, have been less available. And, while it is true, as Gerson points out, that the mere entrance of women into a field does not signal equality (often the fields women enter are quickly downscaled in terms of wages),[7] it remains an important political development.[8] Higher education is significant for our analysis because the very question of women and higher education raises other important questions about the relationship between de facto feminism and the feminist social movement. First, it highlights the political lesson that culture wars only begin when real power becomes an issue. Higher education has consistently been an important dimension of the struggle for economic justice, underscoring the more general point that educational activity provides ever more effective means for effecting continuing progressive social change. As one example, Baxter and Lansing (1983) note that there is a strong intra-gender gap among women with high school educations as opposed to women with college degrees (see the table below).

Table 5.1
The Relationship Between Education and High Interest in Political Campaigns for Women and Men, by Election Year *(Percentage difference)*

Level of Education	Grade School	High School	College
1952	9%	4%	7%
1956	16%	8%	0%
1960	22%	9%	0%
1964	3%	8%	-2%
1968	6%	2%	14%
1972	11%	6%	9%
1976	10%	4%	4%

Source: Baxter and Lansing

In their assessment of this study, Baxter and Lansing noted, among other things, that "Women who attended college expressed virtually the same level of high interest as similar men in four elections out of seven." They further noted that "younger women today are responding differently from older women and are replacing a politically less involved generation" (Baxter and Lansing, 1983: 44-45).

Earlier, we noted that there are many considerations that come into play in discerning what is and is not a political act. The point is this: First, the fact that higher education was a historical and then an actualized feminist goal provides an important window on the study of how feminism happens--through political struggle often in extra-legislative venues. Second, the study indicates the importance of what can broadly be defined as the "political socialization," as a secondary, or derived area of political struggle, the outcome of which is the development of feminist goals among younger women. This second consideration will be considered in detail in the next chapter where we will study how the transmission of feminist goals from one generation to another also has a simultaneous relationship to women's political history.

A number of years ago, my late friend and mentor Professor Mary Edwards, a political scientist, conducted a voluminous series of interviews with working-class women in the Bronx, New York. Her study documented the extent to which their daily concerns were informed by previous and continuing political decision making. It had the effect of highlighting not only the influence of political economy as the primary context, but it highlights the extent to which seemingly nonpolitical decision making and activities were informed by, and in turn influenced, political economy. We can also see this in some of the survey literature. For example, this is evidenced by a survey from the *Fairfield County Advocate*, a regional study that included women from multiethnic and economic groups and a wide range of educational and cultural backgrounds. In the study, women were asked a series of questions, some of which are presented in Table 5.2.

Yet, despite all of these answers, which clearly indicate a feminist *praxis*, and identification with the goals of feminism, women responded to the question: "Do you consider yourself a feminist?" 38 percent affirmative and 58 percent negative (*The Fairfield County Advocate*, 1990). The issue, as far as de facto feminism and the feminist movement is concerned, is the determination of that means by which historically issues have moved from private life into the public sphere and have become subject, not to the ideology of patriarchy, but to *liberal* ideology. Abortion, child care, health care, head-start, divorce, domestic violence, and child support are some of the issues that were once in "the private" and passed over into "the public," becoming social issues, issues that were (and still are) debated along the lines of American liberalism. How these issues were moved and how they were considered on this new liberal basis, in place of the old patriarchal one, is the solution to the paradox.

Table 5.2
Feminist Identification Table

Do you agree with this statement about women?		
Do you agree that women should earn equal pay for equal work?	Yes 97%	No 2%
Do you agree that women *do* earn equal pay for equal work?	Yes 16%	No 82%
Do you think there is a women's movement today?	Yes 87%	No 12%
Would you like to see a future in the U.S. where female executives and presidential candidates are as common as male executives and presidential candidates?	Yes 89%	No 10%
All other things being equal, would you vote for a woman rather than a man?	Yes 60%	No 20%
Is the women's movement getting stronger?	Yes 62%	No 31%

Source: *The Fairfield County Advocate* (July 16, 1990)

What is unique about the philosophy of praxis as political philosophy is that it addresses the age-old problem of the individual and the community in a way that gives a full accounting of the relationship itself, and in the process elucidates a concept of political power that views politics not as something "out there," but, as an operation that is integral to personal existence.

This aspect of power reformulates agency on the basis not just of individual actions, but rather sees individual action as grounding the individual's *relationship* with the community. Our analysis of political economy in this chapter has highlighted that it is this that is the mechanism by which de facto feminism is related to the feminist social movement. In sum, using praxis as an approach underscores the development of political power as something that develops once one has decided to pursue objectives with others, and this is because the context, or totality, is political. Action taken in that context, and decisions rendered in that venue, are internally related to the political context. Another way of putting this is to say that the process by which one engages with others in pursuit of political goals is likewise the process by which one is empowered.

Another approach to this same issue is Ferree and Hess's (1985) work on the new feminist movement where one of their points of focus is the socialization process, and where they maintain that it helps generate what others have termed cognitive praxis. Their work underscores the degree to which the socialization process is itself political. In fact, many of the instances we find in the feminist movement illustrate the degree to which the existence of a feminist social movement *informs* women's assessment of their social situation and generates the world view characteristic of feminism. Some theorists have argued that this new world-view constitutes a resocialization. On the other hand, however, we saw that this is a reciprocal process where the specificity of politics and political demands is informed by daily activity.

The decision by women to view discriminatory working conditions, as is the case in many feminist legal challenges such as we saw in the Johnson Controls Case, as something more than their own personal problem, or problems that express a more limited political distinction (geography, for example), places them in a relationship to the wider social movement that was empowering precisely because of its linkage to previous and ongoing praxes.

One effect of this is to undermine the effects of some features of the socialization process and to place one in contact with one's history. Additionally, as Eyerman and Jamison argue, this is also a process where information, in this case historical information, is translated into a political discourse that is both contemporary to and relevant to the now resocialized individual. *Thus, in effect, one can become resocialized on the basis of one's own praxis.* The upshot of this is that the decision to locate oneself within a wider field of resources, and to view one's situation within a feminist context, and to take on a feminist world view, means that at the level of cognitive praxis, disparate choices are internally related to the feminist movement. As Eyerman and Jamison (1991) put it, it means that one's praxis brings one into a relationship to both the organized and unorganized feminist movement, both historically as well as in terms of present day political realities, and in the process one gains a measure of empowerment.

NOTES

1. See especially Bertell Ollman's account of the philosophy of internal relations, and in particular his depiction of the whole and its parts in *Alienation; Marx's Concept of Man in Capitalist Society* (1978).

2. These arguments surrounding the domestic labor debate, on whether women's work in the home was "productive" (of surplus value) or "unproductive" in the traditional Marxist sense, revolved around whether women were to be considered members of the working class. This created a lengthy debate among Terry Fee and Jane Flax, and Paddy Quick.

3. One could also argue that in the wake of the tumultuous economic forces of the time (mid and late1970s), OPEC, the oil crises, the growing trade deficit, and multinational capitalism's flight to foreign labor platforms, capitalism could not survive unless women continued to perform the functions traditionally assigned to them for free. Unpaid labor in the "home," which serves capitalism by reproducing labor, is considered by some to be the ultimate expression of alienated labor.

4. Although recent analyses have indicated a desire on the part of both the patriarchal state and right-wing anti-feminists to do just that. See Judith Stacey (1982). See also Susan Faludi (1991).

5. This is an important issue and it is addressed by Susan E. Marshall (1991).

6. It is also worth mentioning that women comprise 51.4 percent of the number of people who attend college as second-time students, often over the age of 35. *Atlas of American Women* (1990: 62).

7. Kathleen Gerson (1985: 210) provides additional examples.

8. It is also important to note that the number of Ph.D.'s awarded to women grew during the period between 1972 and 1982 from 16 percent to 32 percent (Gerson 1985: 239).

Chapter 6

De Facto Feminism and Autonomy

We began this inquiry with the history and analysis of the structural reasons why women do not identify with the label feminist. This helped to underscore the paradox of feminism--that women have and do feminism even while bracketing the ideology of feminism. We then turned our focus toward the phenomenon of de facto feminism, something given in experience both in the current literature as well as in the history of the feminist movement. We noted that de facto feminism cannot be fully accounted for on the basis of an ideological approach. Instead, it seemed to require the need for a praxis approach. The analysis of feminist praxis undertaken thus far has shown that de facto feminism has meant something tangible and practical in women's history. It is this that comprises our attempt to formulate the meaning of feminism on a nonideological basis and, in its place, to develop a theory that is grounded in the prior history of feminist praxis. This aspect of praxis, whereby it is a methodology and an epistemology was underscored by Lukacs in his discussion in *History and Class Consciousness* of the manner in which the opacity of being is accounted for by action. It follows from this that the historical reconstruction of the praxis of a social movement, in this case feminism, will also yield the basis on which ontology, in this case the ontology of identity, can proceeded.

What needs to be done at this juncture is to reintroduce some of the earlier categories of analysis (history, structure, and ideology) and view them from the point of the theoretical analysis of the later chapters. This will involve an emphasis on relational ontology when assessing those categories, both at the level of the individual as well as that of the social movement, since this is the content of relational ontology. This undertaking will constitute the procedure for the remaining chapters, the conclusion of which is a formulation of praxis and leadership.

RECONSTRUCTING THE HISTORY OF FEMINISM AS PRAXIS

In Chapter One we considered the origin of the word "feminist" and examined those forces that led to feminism's factionalism as well as its successes. As we saw, the hub around which feminism was so united during the 1910s and which culminated in suffrage was the idea of equality. In the case of suffrage the equality that was sought was political. Yet, this same goal, equality, has been present *since* suffrage. The suffrage victory did not ensure full equality, as underscored by the many legal battles since winning the vote. Generally speaking, the right to property, the fair credit act, and other legislation addressed economic equality. The history of feminism further illustrates the importance attached to freedom as the unhindered access to the development of human potential, or positive freedom (Dietz, 1987: 6). In fact, feminist history supports a particular type of freedom, perhaps best characterized by Susan Carroll as autonomy.[1]

The history of feminism in the twentieth century shows that autonomy was (and is) a major issue and concept.[2] While in recent years it has involved, on the part of de facto feminists, the capacity to choose unorthodox career pathways as well as reproductive control, it is important to point out, as others have, that these are expressions. In fact, it is the mistaking of the expressions of feminism for an ultimate meaning that, as noted earlier, leads to a situation where the expressions are thought to be synonymous *with* feminism.

Autonomy, as a demonstrable predicate of de facto feminism, has never been a "given" for women. Because the concept of autonomy has been opposed by some women (conservative, right-wing activists), we are *not* saying that all women are de facto feminists. Although, as we noted earlier, anti-feminism when expressed by women is self-refuting if one defines feminism along the well-trod lines of freedom and equality. When formulated by a woman, the argument against freedom and equality is beset by those specific contradictions noted by Rousseau centuries earlier--the one thing we are not capable of, or free to do, is to freely deny the exercise of our own will. Freedom, Rousseau tells us, cannot be contradicted at the existential level, and de facto feminism is an indication of that. Nevertheless, at the ideological level, women's history in the twentieth century indicates that there have been specific women who were, and specific women who were not, feminists. What we can also say is that the praxis of autonomy, which is the essence of de facto feminism, has its point of origin not in ideology, but in the conflict with an objective material condition. It follows from this that ideological attacks on de facto feminism that do not address these fundamental material condition of existence are but abstractions.

Throughout history a distinguishable predicate of feminism can be identified, that is, autonomy defined as both a freedom from restrictive patriarchal structures and mores as well as the capacity to pursue economic independence. This idea was not imposed on our analysis in an a priori fashion. Instead, the specific history of feminism in America, when viewed from the perspective of praxis, illustrates that the struggle for autonomy and the understanding of autonomy were constant throughout the time period. For, when we ask the question, "What does it mean to be a feminist?" an answer is provided by looking at the *actions* of de facto feminists, or what feminism has accomplished through and in history.

Theoretically, the inability of some of the current approaches to feminism to account for the actual historical manner in which change was accomplished or the issue of inclusion was a major shortcoming of the ideological formulations of feminism. Feminist theory arrives at a completely different perspective on feminism, one which includes a more accurate account of the history of feminism itself, where praxis is used as a methodology. This is, to a certain extent, counter intuitive. For, in the first instance it appears that an understanding of feminism would require first and foremost a catalogue of attributes that distinguishes those who say they *are* feminists from those who say that they are *not*. In fact this approach yields exactly that problem which modern feminism is entrenched in: an overemphasis on consciousness. As a result, many analyses leave out a considerable number of women *and* their activities. It is for this reason that emphasis needs to be placed instead on women's agency, or on what they in fact *do*. When this is emphasized through history, the choices women make reflect both equality with men and greater freedom--and the research indicates that making these choices through and in history have brought about the achievement of feminist goals. Of course, individual counterexamples are always available. When viewed from the level of society, and when assessing change as it actually comes about (nonabstractly), individuals who are held out as counterexamples are placed in a more appropriate context.

If we turn toward more recent feminist history the central issue of autonomy once again surfaces, but this time against the backdrop of substantive, society wide political accomplishments. However, this has taken place within the context of the attempt to reestablish patriarchal control over women's reproductive rights. Control over reproductive rights has been and is a key ideological and political position of patriarchy. We can see the importance of praxis if we look again at the issue of autonomy as it surfaced in the example of the Webster decision. Here, there are two points that should be underscored. First, the large number of women who protested against Webster were unaccounted for by traditional assessments of women's political strength. Secondarily, we saw that there was some suggestion that this underestimation owed to the dominance of consciousness in attitudinal surveys and measurement techniques within political science (Donahue, 1996). There is, however, a third contributing factor--the persistence of a social ontology which limits a priori the scope of human experience.

Any discussion of the ontology of de facto feminism raises the epistemological question: "How do we know that this is the case?" While a complete development of what would constitute a feminist epistemology is beyond our scope, some of the operative epistemological considerations should be considered. Here we will borrow from Marx the idea that history is self-grounding, which is, in Marx's vernacular, class struggle. Therefore, for Marx, it is working-class praxis that defines truth, a truth that itself emerged from the specific actions of the working class in pursuit of its self-interest (Ball, 1977: 7). In developing this, Marx posited ideology as the attempt to obfuscate the truth and to formulate *false* interests for *self*-interest. The relevance of this to this chapter, therefore, is the procedure for deriving the meaning of feminism from the actions of feminists. Thus, we are seeking to ground feminism in something that is itself self-grounding, namely feminist praxis.

This method of analysis places a greater emphasis upon the actual *history* of feminist activity as opposed to belief systems or cultural considerations, which often reflect back upon the depiction of feminist history, often viewing it after the political struggle had already established institutional, cultural, and educational forms.

While these considerations are not insignificant, neither are they insurmountable (and it is true that groups and individual action can always be open to the suggestion that they are colored by such cultural factors). In determining whether a pragmatic standard for an action conforms to the goals of the movement, the only question that remains is: "Did that activity contribute to the development of feminism or not?" The question then arises, How do we account for the transmission of feminism from the point of view of politics?

In fact, Joyce Gelb and Marian Palley (1978: 362-392), by introducing the contribution of Schattschneider to feminism, help to answer this question. When we ask: How do feminist values become transmitted from one generation to another and from one group to another? Or, more specifically: How does *autonomy* become accepted as a goal? The answer seems to lie in Schattschneider's work, which only by abstraction can be separated from the previous praxis that brought it into being in the first place. E. E. Schattschneider characterized "politics as the socialization of conflict" (the process whereby conflict is routinized and woven into the institutional behavior of the state and interest groups, as well as the way in which the expectations and behavior of individuals are structured by the existing societal rules) (1956: 39). This characterization provides a point of contact between ontology and politics.

In seeking to account for the meaning of politics, Schattschneider developed several other concepts that also became classics in political science. However, it is his contention that politics involves "organizing in" and "organizing out" (the process whereby politics means that some groups are included by virtue of their being in the position of greater or lesser relative wealth, and some are excluded because of various bureaucratic mechanisms and subjective expectations), as well as his notion of the "mobilization of bias" (the idea that political conflict is a permanent and necessary part of social life, and that the bias in society represents the preorganized or the potential of politics), which provides an answer to the question: How are the goals of feminism transmitted?

The attempt to apply Schattschneider to feminism means that we are formulating the position that feminist goals (through an initial and explicit political struggle) have become part of the societal bias. We could also say, for reasons we will consider shortly, that feminist identity and the label feminist lies outside of the bias. This is one explanation of the paradox of modern feminism, and it seems to provide a complete answer to the question of how feminist goals have been transmitted from one generation to the next without the acceptance of the label feminist, even during periods of time when consciousness-raising was not taking place.

It might be useful to provide an example of how the use of Schattschneider's formulation relates to the example of a specific feminist goal that we considered in our last chapter--women's access to higher education. We will examine the phenomenon of women's pursuit of higher education as an achieved goal of feminism, and then view it from the perspective of the ontology of praxis.

In the first instance, this goal (higher education) became assimilated into and accepted within the societal bias. As successive generations came onto the scene in American society, they were socialized into an acceptance of a general cluster of ideas and beliefs that influenced and ultimately became a part of the societal bias. At a certain point in history, women's education became a part of this cluster of ideas and beliefs.

This was supported by liberal ideology, the dominant public philosophy in the United States, through the particular ideal of equality of opportunity for women as "individuals." Finally, in terms of history, when enough of the feminist program--its specific goal of equality and other goals--were assimilated into social life, those who accept the overall public philosophy, in general, *are accepting feminism as a consequence of that belief and adherence.* Thus, to a certain extent, feminism at this juncture would have less to do with acceptance or rejection of feminism per se than it would have to do with their existence in a specific political economy and its socialization patterns. For example, twenty-five years ago only one in four members in law schools were women. Today, 40 percent of law students are women.[3]

The actual historical record supports this interpretation. During the late nineteenth century, when a small number of predominantly upper-class women were graduating from college, there were few jobs for them upon graduation. Yet, their eventual work in emerging social service organizations, in settlement houses, and hospitals provided the actual impetus and legitimization for women to pursue higher education in larger numbers (O'Neill, 1969: 90-95). It is clear from what has been said that some form of introduction to and agreement with "equality of opportunity," either implicitly or explicitly, is a precondition for de facto feminism since the idea of de facto feminism is inconceivable without activity that affirms this idea. Obviously, for example, the 51.4 percent (*Atlas of American Women*, 1987: 63) of women currently pursuing higher education would not be doing so if they did not feel they had that particular right in liberal society. When we examine "equality of opportunity," however, it transits from being merely a liberal mantra toward being what Zillah Eisenstein (1981) saw in it--the radical idea of freedom for women in the context of patriarchy, which for our purposes here, may be thought of as a socialization pattern.

Early women's rights activists such as Mary Wollstonecraft and, later, Elizabeth Cady Stanton and other activists were deeply committed to women's entrance into and success in higher education. It was, therefore, from the very outset a clearly defined goal and an immediate high priority. Indeed, when women's history is examined from the perspective of women and higher education in America, one is struck at once with its success: women have clearly achieved parity in education in terms of numbers.[4]

But how is it that these changes in women's educational status, eagerly sought and worked for by previous generations of women, continued to be supported during periods when feminism was widely considered to have been in decline, indeed, even during some periods when social progress itself was on trial?

Before proceeding further we should consider a similar, but profoundly different idea--it is the academy that is the vehicle whereby feminism is introduced and continued from one generation to the next. This idea would mean that only women who attended college during a specific time frame are responsible for the development of de facto feminism. However, we clearly saw that in fact this type of grassroots feminism is enhanced and developed on a daily basis through activity largely outside of the academy as well. Bookman and Morgan, for example, illustrate how working-class women, while rejecting the feminist label, have embraced political concerns that fall within the repertoire of feminism. These women can also come to understand, and reject patriarchal domination as they organize around issues that are not solely "women's issues-the gender consciousness that emerges in working-class women's lives involves an active negotiation between the prevailing and the oppositional ideologies available to them. They make sense of these contending ideas, including feminism, in *terms* of the material condition of their lives" (Bookman and Morgan, 1988: 11-12). Consequently, the success of women in the academy, even their theoretical success, is a result of previous praxis. It is true that the progressive socialization of the nineteenth and early twentieth centuries were initiated by college-educated women, however, to ignore working-class women's contribution during the same time frame, either in their experiences in the West or in labor unions, is to miss entirely the participatory nature of social freedom.

As stated earlier, the history of women's education also evidences that after initial difficulties, women's right to higher education was widely accepted and eventually became a part of the landscape of social life. By tracing the success of women in education--through its development in theorists such as Wollstonecraft, to the establishment of women's colleges, and finally to current educational parity--the answer to this question can be examined in more detail. In terms of setting dates, O'Neill notes that "Few women received a good education before the Civil War, but by 1870 eleven thousand women were enrolled in some 528 institutions of higher learning" (O'Neill, 1969: 13).

The specific idea that women should go to college, and that it was a good idea for society for them to do so became part of the bias to the point where today it is merely assumed and taken for granted. Likewise, in the case of feminist goal after feminist goal, we find that, after political struggle and praxis, the goal becomes a part of the political culture and comprises an aspect of the societal bias. The already established patterns that we see then cannot serve as a point of origin for a discussion of either how these changes came about, let alone assessments about their ultimate nature.

The point to be stressed is that, like other aspects of feminism, the case of women and higher education is a paradigm that indicates that feminism, to a large degree, has been accepted *in fact* and as a consequence of earlier and often continuing feminist praxis. It is, at the same time, a process whereby many ideological debates of long standing have become, as we saw in the example of women in the military, irrelevant. Ontologically, these changes are also grounded in the facticity of women themselves, which refers to the irreducible quality of individual existence as the point of origin for social change, or a theory of social change. Having examined and introduced "autonomy" within the context of an ontology of praxis, it may be useful to do the same with our research into the family and political economy.

DE FACTO FEMINISM, CLASS, AND THE POLITICAL ECONOMY OF THE FAMILY

Earlier in the discussion of Barbara Bergmann's work, *The Economic Emergence of Women*, we focused on Bergmann's grounding of the movement for women's liberation in empirical, as opposed to ideological, factors. Bergmann's work was ground-breaking, not only because of her conclusions, but also because of her use of political economy. Her work circumvented the usual ideological debate surrounding feminism and arrived at an objective, nonideological explanation for the continuation of the effort for women's equal rights in America--the factual presence of large numbers of women in the labor force. Ultimately, for the purposes of this analysis, what is of the greatest interest in Bergmann's study is not the secondary discourse concerning the need to work, but the materialism that is implied in her analysis. Specifically, what is noteworthy for a discussion of feminist praxis and identity is the idea that the point of origin for feminist praxis is an engagement with an initial set of empirical facts, as opposed to ideology. However, in our discussion of women's history we have continued to emphasize feminist praxis as the ultimate basis for that empirical fact.

Another way of approaching the question of the ontology of de facto feminism is through Gould's discussion of the perennial problem of the individual and the community. Gould conceives of individuals in a "relational" context and manages to recast the historical debate over the individual versus the community as a priori connected to others. As she puts it: "the individuals are therefore ontologically primary, but the relations among them are also essential aspects of their being" (Gould, 1988: 105).

To put the matter another way, the individual needs to be represented as having a considerable number of connections to institutions, structures, groups, and other individuals. It is a more expansive portrait of the individual. The process whereby these connections exist through time, as well as the connections themselves, need to be viewed as every bit a part of the individual (Gould, 1988: 105-106).

Earlier, we noted that the relationship of the individual to the socioeconomic order takes place against the backdrop of a socialization process. This process works *for* women's mediated relationship to the socioeconomic goods of society (patriarchy), even while the ideology (liberalism) of the economic system itself works to undermine patriarchal socialization patterns.

What is more important for this analysis than the conflict between opposing ideologies is the facticity implied by the ontology of praxis, which is illustrated by the fact that de facto feminist *praxis* works toward, on the one hand, a different socialization pattern, and on the other, an empirical erosion of patriarchy through daily activity and decision making. To illustrate this point, it might be useful to recall Bergmann's explication of the way the economic ordering of society leads toward such a praxis. In the first instance, according to Bergmann, the economy gives rise to an increase in the value of women's labor time and, in the second instance, this material set of circumstances is translated into a set of behaviors (and eventually, new socialization patterns).

Finally, the empirical basis of women's praxis resurfaces in such a way that, even while being socialized into a mediated relationship to the socioeconomic order (through men and the family), they become resocialized on the basis of their own praxis.

This is one way to characterize how that praxis becomes the ontological basis of de facto feminism. It is in this sense that we can return to what we set out earlier as a goal--Marx's idea of history as self-grounding. In the case of de facto feminism we have emphasized that the process by which de facto feminism is grounded is immanent to itself and is expressed as such when we say that women are resocialized on the basis of their own praxis.

Still another way of looking at this is to say that an individual women's relationship to the economic and social order is also a relationship to feminist history. Having said that de facto feminism has come about historically through the presence of feminist goals within the societal bias, one element of this ontology needs to be a woman's relationship to feminist history by way of redeveloped socialization patterns. Here we are referring to Bergmann's point regarding the direct effect of working outside the home (in the exterior workplace) on both consciousness and social change.

We can examine this conflict from the point of view of Betty Friedan's. We can depict one aspect of the "problem with no name" as an awareness, at some level, among women of the conflict between the old ideology of patriarchy as it related to their role in the home and the economy, and the achievement of a feminist goal, namely that they were college educated (Friedan, 1963). This conflict can be described also as one between staying at home or working outside the home where women's labor, according to Bergmann, is more highly valued.

It is in this case that one notices the self-informing nature of praxis. Many women who were opposed to feminist goals (by virtue of their socialization into an acceptance of patriarchal ideology) changed that position by their praxis in the external labor force or by coming into contact with the realities of life in patriarchal society, as opposed to the myths by which patriarchy reproduces itself. They were thus enabled to overcome that form of cognitive dissonance that characterizes the "feminine mystique."

Bergmann makes a compelling case that the changes brought about by women's entrance into the non domestic economy, a development that spanned decades and parallels the feminist movement, wrought these considerable changes in women's lives. When speaking of political economy we are using it in a broad sense, including within it women's autonomy.

However, the use of the philosophy of praxis means that "the economy" or "the economic order" are to a certain extent abstractions vis-a-vis autonomy, that is, it has only an abstract life aside from the praxis of the people who comprise it. Thus, when the economy is cited as an agent of change, in every instance it implies individual and/or aggregate human agency, and women's entrance and growth in the labor force was the end result of generations of previous praxes. Just as a feminist culture is the outcome of previous praxes and not a point of origin, so too with the labor force participation of women. Precisely because Bergmann can speak of a *history* of women and the economy, the first reference must be to women's agency and praxis. To miss this crucial distinction is to attribute to the economy and, consequently, to women's economic emergence a necessity that it does not possess.

The philosophy of praxis maintains that only the actions of specific human wills, either acting in concert or alone, can bring about those events that in every instance presuppose human agency. However, in discussing human agency and the individual, it is also important to keep in mind Gould's formulation of ontology, with its emphasis on human beings as primarily *relational*. Thus, it may be useful to examine the issue of class as it relates to de facto feminism, since class is the category that modifies statements regarding individual agency.

DE FACTO FEMINISM AND CLASS

The relationship between the individual and the socialization process is important for an ontology of feminism because it establishes women's relationship not only to the society in which they live, but to women's history as well. This history, referred to once by Merleau-Ponty as the "in-between" (of subject and object) of human existence, contains all those victories and struggles that have been assimilated into the socialization process as axiomatic in political and social life. The historical dimensions of the ontology of feminism then contribute toward an explanation of how it is that feminism has continued and has been assimilated from one generation to the next in the absence of very many self-identified feminists, or even when feminism itself seemed to be in decline. It is through the individual's relationship to the society's political culture, and thereby to history, that this tradition continues. Women are connected to feminist history and the diverse feminist conflicts within women's history, such as the debate over legal and reproductive rights, education, fair credit, and equal pay, through their relationship to the political culture and the public philosophy established through the socialization process.[5]

What it means to be a feminist implies that the primary relationship is that of an individual woman to her history. This relationship can be represented, as can all relational processes, as a continuum along either positive or negative lines, and as either supporting or rejecting aspects of feminism (for example, its goals) that are reflected in women's history.

There are many examples of de facto feminist choices that place them in a relationship to feminist history: the pursuit of lifestyles that reflect or imply a negation of patriarchal values, increasing emphasis on exercising power, raising children in a nonsexist way, building cooperative as opposed to competitive relationships with other women, and the insistence on shared efforts in the reproduction of life's necessities so as to have more time and energy available to engage in what Arendt referred to as "the life of action." The list of such de facto feminist actions is as long as there are situations women are likely to be in during the course of a day, ranging from the most mundane to the most exceptional.

The historical aspect of the ontology of feminism then, should be understood in terms of an agency that offers a middle ground between economic determinism on the one hand, and the inculcation of ideology on the other. Choices that reflect a positive relationship toward the history of feminism, as we find to be the case with de facto feminists, affirm and structure the relationship of women to their history.

Earlier, our analysis of feminist identity and women's history underscored the role of ideology and the way in which ideology is circumvented, even subverted, by feminist praxis. The analysis undertaken so far raises the need to determine what the "real" conflict is between feminism and its opponents. In fact, what emerges from the historical analysis is that the concept which forms the basis of Marshall's "Who Speaks for American Women," Flexner's *Century of Struggle* is a pivotal one. These two works address the question: "What or whom did feminists struggle against as evidenced from the analysis of women's history?" Patriarchal opposition was exercised, in this view, through organizations and institutions that had a clear political stake at issue. Some feminist scholars note (Marshall, 1991; Marilley, 1989) that there was an organizational and institutional continuity among the opponents of both first and second waves of feminism.

One area of feminist scholarship that has continued to be of interest in this regard is the relationship between feminism and class. One example that scholars have focused on is the socialization of young girls to the myth of "Prince Charming." In this familiar scenario, a young girl is lifted from a life of poverty and placed in a fantasyland where everything is provided for in exchange for her performing her appointed sexual and personal roles. The theme itself has been a recurring one in patriarchal ideology, but the critique of it has developed concurrently. In literature, this theme has often been portrayed powerfully, most notably perhaps in Ibsen's *A Doll's House,* where Nora has a moment of recognition of her demeaning status and makes a dramatic break for autonomy. To the extent that this is a component of the socialization process in American society, women are ideologically conditioned to expect privilege as an objective condition.

The issue of class is at the heart of the myth even though the myth itself goes a long way toward masking this issue. The myth has the effect of hiding the class position of women, even while admitting class as an abstract category. The myth of Prince Charming does not say or imply that class doesn't exist, but rather that by dint of exceptional behavior, or just plain good fortune, one can become a "special" person and thereby escape class all together.

Class position then is actually employed in the myth in order to give it that requisite amount of fear that will transform it from a fable that is seemingly harmless into a functioning aspect of political socialization. It is then, in this light that we can appreciate the full force of the attacks that accompany feminist insistence upon exposing the lie. It is frequently attacked with extreme ire by advocates of patriarchy, and this can be detected most notably in many of its spokespeople, who often complain that feminists only want to spoil the fun for everyone (Marshall, 1984).

All of this underscores the need for even greater attention to the politics surrounding this ideological conflict. Ultimately, the point is the insistence on the distinction between myth and reality. There exists a severe dissonance between ideology and "realpolitik" in America on this issue. The stark reality is not that which is portrayed by the myth of "prince charming," but the actual class position of women as illustrated by the "the feminization of poverty."

It is, however, in the disassembling of myth from reality that an important aspect of de facto feminism, namely that *de facto feminism is a realism,* emerges. Feminists are the target of such vehemence precisely because feminism means an "owning up" to the reality that universal, inherited empty class status is a ruse, and that class is a fact, and that many features of patriarchal ideology are an affirmation of class. Thus, some of the anger directed at feminists has to do with its realism and the role it plays in disclosing women's actual relationship to class.

In this view, feminism would be an accurate appraisal of women's situation coupled with a strategy and praxis to promote one's self on the basis of her individual existence. Facing up to the economic facts for women means overcoming the socialization of the myth of prince charming and the recognition of the importance, even if implicitly, of the effects of political economy.

At what point an individual woman makes the judgment that she must confront this form of alienation is related to specific conditions and involves considerations that are the province of other academic disciplines (chiefly psychology and sociology). However, *that* it takes place cannot be doubted, and that disclosing that it takes place is precisely the role of a phenomenological inquiry.

Whereas patriarchal ideology is intended to create a dissonance with social and existential reality, de facto feminism and its praxis are the expressions of actual needs. The politics of de facto feminism, when viewed in contrast to patriarchal ideology, places ideology in a contradictory position to autonomy. This is one of the reasons why it is important to focus on activity, instead of limiting the analysis to consciousness when examining feminist identity. It is simply not consistent with the literature to suggest that feminism is merely a matter of information, of simply, for example, imparting feminist consciousness to those who lack it. While we are not discounting the ideological dimensions (as indicated by our discussion of the myth of prince charming), the statement that de facto feminism is a realism implies that there is an actual, tangible political conflict that is at issue.

Some of the most common descriptions of this conflict have centered on issues such as level of education or political identity. However, the criterion we are addressing--that it involves an actual conflict in experience-- seems to suggest that something nonideological is at work. The point is that the criterion suggested requires a complex understanding of class. For example, what is the class position of a wholly dependent woman married to a wealthy man? Class position is far too problematic in the case of feminism, not only because of the difficulties surrounding the institution of the family, but because, traditional female socialization works to undermine explicit identity with other women thus making it difficult to approach class without accounting for these extensive mediations. One of these mediations is that the traditional socialization process provides a vehicle for escaping one's class status primarily through the above mentioned prince charming scenario. The prince charming scenario usually means that the prince is upper class. Yet, while class position per se, or class in the traditional sense, is not directly translatable into de facto feminist identity, something *approximating* class is clearly at issue.

We can however, approach the issue of class through the study of autonomy. Autonomy is a key aspect of feminist activity and has been strongly correlated with economic independence from individual men. This has been directly translated into political preferences (voting and candidate performance evaluation) indicating either a difference among women who are existentially independent of individual men, including economic and psychological independence (Carroll, 1989). Autonomy, being a direct contradiction of patriarchy would, it seems, acts as a countervailing force to that of patriarchy as an ideology. We can see the influence of the mediations on class regarding women if we examine Carroll's examples, where the presence of autonomy highlights the mediations that exist for women who are or have become independent from individual men, either psychologically (through parenting, education, and other avenues of independent thinking), or economically, by working outside the home. One way to express this is to state that the historical development of autonomy is perhaps a precondition for class analysis. Where it is lacking as an objective condition that is studied, it must be accounted for by the theory that intends to examine it.

A lack of theoretical support for autonomy, even for the purpose of emphasizing class solidarity, actually has the effect of undermining the subsequent use of class analysis, and whatever accomplishments are brought about by subsuming or by-passing autonomy are likely to be short lived. The politics of feminist history can be viewed as a twofold process in which women's autonomy is enhanced as individual development even while creating greater potential as members of a class.

De facto feminists, whose presence signaled the need for the rethinking of feminist identity undertaken here, are the cornerstone for understanding the relationship between autonomy and class, or at another level, between the individual and the community, where the relationship between the individual and the community is mediated by a question of identity. In effect, de facto feminism represents a phenomenological verification of Eisenstein's thesis regarding the radical future of liberal feminism and provides the possibility of a truly multiethnic, multicultural questioning of social relationships. As we saw, de facto feminism is an undermining of patriarchal ideology or those aspects of it that touch upon the lives of individual actors who happen to be de facto feminists, but it also signals the tremendous importance of *praxis* as a category of analysis for feminist political theory. Thus, it reverses the limiting effect of precisely those mediations that have undermined class (ideology, consciousness, belief systems, etc.). However, it also underscores how difficult it is to approach the question of class directly in the case of women. It is a difficulty that owes not only to ideology, but to mediation, and most especially the mediating effects of the family.

The "fact" in de facto feminism is meant to convey that de facto feminism is a *realism*. The emphasis is thereby shifted to the importance de facto feminism has for the emotional and physical development of women (de facto feminists). De facto feminism addresses not just an ideological pursuit of the goals of feminism but, first and foremost (since it is realized on the basis of praxis), it is an actual political pursuit involving the initiation and continuity of a political *conflict,* the telos of which is the dissolution of patriarchy. What is of greater importance however, is that the specific pursuit of the goals of feminism by de facto feminists is a consequence of a more primary sense of urgency on their part. This is expressed, as we saw, by their actions, but it is most universally captured by their status as the living awareness of the "the feminization of poverty."

The phrase itself indicates the seriousness of the political stakes for de facto feminists. To put it another way, "the feminization of poverty" presupposes the real, practical, and nonideological character of the politics of de facto feminism. On this score, there have been a number of interviews in the popular media where the contingency of women's class position is highlighted by women who had accepted the traditional family scenario and were wholly dependent upon their husbands for the support of themselves and their children, but who were subsequently left on their own either by divorce or separation. These interviews ended with the statement by the interviewee that women all need to pursue their own individual self-interest (as politics) against the backdrop of the *feminization of poverty.*

Therefore, what was said earlier regarding feminism as a realism can also be approached from the point of view of the political self-interest of de facto feminists. De facto feminism, when viewed from the perspective of praxis as rational self-interest in action, underscores the fact that at the root of this praxis is the very real threat of poverty. It is the presence of this reality that enables de facto feminist praxis to over-ride ideology and the socialization of privilege. It is also this reality that provides the linkage to class analysis, with the important mediations we have outlined.

NOTES

1. Susan Carroll's definition of autonomy is best described as political autonomy, or: "as the quality or state of being self-governing, independent in political decision making" (Carroll, 1990: 240). Our definition here is a broader one that includes a freedom from restrictive patriarchal structures and values as well as the capacity to pursue authenticity--the fullest development of one's self as an individual.

2. For a more detailed discussion of this concept see Hester Eisenstein (1983: 67) and Maggie Humm, (1990: 14-15).

3. Remarks by Betty Fridan on C-Span regarding the progress of women in American politics, January 19, 1997.

4. Obviously, discrimination still exists at the level of professional practice (women hired and promoted to full time or full professor rank). Also, discrimination with a discipline makes it difficult for women entering the natural sciences such as physics.

5. Ted Lowi's work, *The End of Liberalism*, deals expressly with the issue of the politics that is implied by the very existence of a public philosophy.

Chapter 7

Conclusion: The Emergence of De Facto Feminism as Political Leadership

De facto feminism, when examined from the perspective of the phenomenological analysis undertaken thus far, has highlighted the practical activities of women as they have engaged with the major forces that structure their existence. One aspect of this has been our focus on the contribution of de facto feminists toward the development of feminism and the dismantling of patriarchy.

The very scope of the activities of de facto feminists has led many popular commentators on feminism to complain about the areas de facto feminists have challenged--the family, child-rearing, and, in short, the reproduction of social relationships at the level, and in the manner, that they deem necessary. These challenges, since they amount to a detailed and ground-up expression of personal politics, have been considerable, cumulative, and widespread. The pace and scope of change that de facto feminism has brought to American society is remarkable for this central fact--it encompasses all of those personal areas and public spaces that were once informed, or continue to be informed, by patriarchy. This can be witnessed on a daily basis on many conservative radio talk shows where hosts complain the most bitterly about the changes wrought by "those feminists."

It has been a cliche to note that any dissolution, even ones that are positive like the dissolution of patriarchy, are woeful to behold. But that has not been the case with de facto feminism, even though the contributions of de facto feminists to the quality and stability of American society and politics has been greatly overlooked.

Because patriarchy is a political pathology, the activities of de facto feminists are ultimately activities that heal the body politic, not ones that injure it. This is because the routinized abuse of power, grounded in an antiquarian assertion of politics and reproduced on the basis of economic convenience and ideology, has led to the notorious litany of contradictions that have themselves been the subject of numerous recent treatises.

Also, since patriarchy is so clearly aligned with the socialization process, it has seemed that the emphasis of de facto feminists on discussing and explicating the relevant personal moments of that process has amounted to an overly introspective self. For example, detractors often point to the extent to which de facto feminists view therapy as a normal course of dealing with everyday problems. But in many cases these problems arise from a socialization process beset by the pathology of patriarchy. Taken as a whole, the combined effect of this introspection, which often results after engaging with the power differentials immanent to patriarchal society, has been to improve the quality of political discourse and life in America.

The ability to communicate and to understand one's self is well on its way to becoming a universal value in America, even while strength, brute force, and rhetoric, either in personal or national political life, are being delegitimized. Nowhere is this lesson made clearer than in the influence of de facto feminists on leadership. A feminist style of leadership has recently emerged, and it is one that not only illustrates the shortcomings of the other previously dominant models--that of the corporate model of hierarchy and the national political model patterned on the American presidency--but also includes a normative dimension based on its greater efficacy. That normative dimension is the emphasis it places on inclusion and communication, and it is precisely this that has helped to undermine the patriarchal component in other models.

This final chapter, therefore, will examine the different styles of leadership and explicate the emerging feminist model, which has been brought into existence by the everyday activities of women whom, for the purposes of this book, I have termed de facto feminists. It underscores in a quite convincing way the central fact of this part of our analysis--that the dissolution of patriarchy brought on by de facto feminist praxis has also brought with it a positive normative contribution at every turn. The initiation of a style of leadership to fill the void left by the dissolution of the patriarchal model is intended to be a case in point.

In recent years there have been a number of important contributions to the study of leadership. Many of them have provided students of leadership with the tools necessary to analyze the strengths and weaknesses of existing leadership models. The valuable insights gained from these studies have underscored the distinct qualities of an emergent feminist model of leadership. Briefly, the models we will consider here are the presidential model of national leadership, the corporate (traditional) model, and the emergent form of feminist leadership. The latter, as we will show, was not imposed from without, but developed out of the course of women engaging with the situations that they confronted within organizations, either public or private.

Where weaknesses are identified in the first two models, I want to stress the role of patriarchy as contributing to their ineffectiveness, as well as how the feminist contribution corrects these shortcomings. I want to focus on the patriarchal source of the weakness so that some preliminary judgments can be made about how the emerging feminist approach overcomes these difficulties.

I should begin my analysis by acknowledging the uneasiness that pervades many feminist discussions of leadership. At a colloquium I attended recently, the very mention or prospect of the word "leader" in a talk on feminist theory met with strong disapproval from some in attendance. However, as I hope to show, the activities of de facto feminism regarding leadership has had the result of overcoming what are, in essence, reservations about inequality that linger around the word "leader." An additional reason for this discomfort with discussions of leadership involve the feminist critique of hierarchy so often associated with leadership, and the sentiments feminist theory shares with forms of participatory democracy. In the national political arena, this uneasiness (particularly in the media) often takes the form of a level of distrust and skepticism concerning leadership.[1]

Political leadership at the national level, however, offers us an important window on identifying those forces and structures that have recently brought into question the very possibility of leadership per se in the contemporary era.

THE DISSOLUTION OF PATRIARCHAL ELEMENTS WITHIN
THE PRESIDENTIAL MODEL OF NATIONAL LEADERSHIP

The field of presidential politics is rife with the ideas that support a "traditional" style of leadership, one associated with masculinity and premised on characteristics like "strength." Presidential leadership and politics, therefore, provide us with an opportunity to analyze both the traditional style of leadership as well as the structural forces at work in its demise. This is significant because the emergent feminist leadership model is suited for the new context in that it meets and successfully manages these same structural forces.

As the pinnacle of political leadership in American politics, the American presidency typically follows a hierarchical chain of command approach to leadership. Throughout American history, presidential leadership has been equated with strength, and strength has often meant domination.

A number of presidential scholars (Lowi, Buchanan, and Nelson) have drawn attention to the difficulties created by an overemphasis upon the characteristic of strength when analyzing presidential leadership. Specifically, it creates a set of expectations that Ted Lowi, for one, considers self-defeating. "First, having given presidents maximum power to govern and all the help they ever asked for, the public has rationally focused its expectations on them, counting on them to deliver on all the promises they explicitly made"(1985: 20). In effect, expectations based on strength, the ability to brings one's personal weight to bear on a set of problems, are incompatible with the realities of congressional politics, the competitive forces of the modern media, and a political culture marked, above all else, by a high degree of skepticism.

There is also the contradiction between political expectations based on this socially constructed equation of strength and leadership and the realities of the process of governance wherein the president, as H. Mark Roelofs notes, is a "surprisingly weak player" (1992: 117).

One need only think back to the first Clinton inauguration to see the limitations of this style of strength-based leadership and its abject failure in all its grandeur. No sooner had candidate Clinton been transformed into President Clinton, standing on the steps of the Lincoln Monument, the very picture of the "strong, charismatic leader," than talk was already surfacing about a "failed presidency." Given Clinton's reelection, the protean assessments that are proffered by commentators are unlikely to be stilled by a cessation of media hubris.

The point is that questions have been raised about this strength-based model of leadership. Can this style of leadership be maintained? Or, have conditions that once allowed this style of leadership been changed forever? A case in point is the erosion of a presidential private sphere wherein the larger-than-life image of a strong leader can be both formulated and maintained. The modern media have managed to break down all of the barriers that had previously prevented the public from gaining access to the president's private life. It seems that the line between what is considered public knowledge and private information has been blurred forever. The media inform the public about all aspects of the president's personal life. In this atmosphere, is it possible to retain the "myth" that supports the idea of a strong, superman president?

Additionally, the takeover fever that swept through the networks during the 1980s means that networks now compete with one another in their search for the "best dirt." Together, advances in technology and the proliferation of media venues, which make it possible to contradict a president's words and actions almost instantaneously by simultaneously presenting current and past proclamations (which may be contradictory) on a split screen, highlight the president's and other national political leaders' foibles, and further undercuts the ability of a leader to maintain a "strong" image.

Among structural causes, the modern mass media are not the only forces driving these changes. Other structural changes that took place during the 1970s (growing lack of support for the president, and changes in presidential primaries) have served to undercut the ability of presidents to project and maintain a strong image. During the 1980s a number of changes arose--the explosive growth of tabloid-style TV programs, the economies of media mergers and the prevalence of a merging of news and entertainment. Taken en masse, these changes make reliance upon the characteristic of strength as a leadership style, premised as it was on a zone of privacy (which allowed myth making to continue), simply untenable in the current political environment. At the same time that the decline of the traditional style of leadership was taking place, there was also an emerging feminist style. Increasingly, the traditional model has come to be seen as irrational because, I would argue, of the greater openness, communication, and emphasis on consensus that has marked this emerging feminist model. Viewed in contrast to feminist praxis, the patriarchal models of leadership often appear ineffective and groundless, at best and capricious at worst.

The changes that have undermined the efficacy of strength-based, patriarchal leadership can be applied not only to the president but to other national political venues as well. In instance after instance, attempts to establish authority on the basis of a patriarchal strength-based leadership style have ultimately led to an undermining of the person in question and, in some cases, a questioning of the legitimacy of the office as well. Much of the traditional, and even some of the contemporary, discourse on leadership is replete with references to a natural order which seems out of place in contemporary approaches to the question of leadership. One of the difficulties here, of course, is that a "natural" form of leadership is unverifiable since presumably the recorded past is also the socially constructed past, and unless one is attuned to the social construction of reality, what one thinks one is describing as "natural" could instead simply be the outcome of the socialization process operating in history.

Nowhere is this more apparent than in discussions of the strong leader. The strong leader has been constructed to have as its point of reference the ability to make the "tough decisions," presumably the decision to annihilate scores of civilians, for example. Or else, the strong leader is held up to refer to the striving after megalomaniacal control over others, and one is a strong leader to the degree to which one is able to subjugate others.

The problem lies in the social construction of the strong leader. Strong leaders are, after all, those who are already in a position of leadership, and it is this prepositioning of the individual, a prepositioning that takes place separate and apart from the processes by which they are there in the first place, that makes the social construction of the strong leader a theoretical as well as a practical problem. As Austin and Leland note, one common thread running through many of the traditional models of leadership is that there is an overemphasis on "positional leaders." In their view, a bias (resulting from "social construction") takes place whereby the study of leaders--who are already in a position of leadership --grounds the model of leadership on these qualities as though their position had nothing to do with the possession of those qualities in the first instance (Austin and Leland, 1991).

THE CORPORATE MANAGEMENT MODEL OF LEADERSHIP

A second style of leadership has been undermined by its patriarchal components. Here, the difficulty is not only the emphasis on strength (as in the strong man and his tactics), but the overemphasis on goals over process, which is itself a hallmark of patriarchy. Both of these additional elements of patriarchy undermine its effectiveness as a leadership style.

Recent scholarship on corporate leadership has focused upon a dichotomized approach to the study of leadership, breaking it down to a style known   generically as "traditional" (transactional) and an alternative "interactive" or "transformational" model (Applebaum and Shapiro, 1993). These models further break down along gender lines where the traditional is considered male and the interactive is viewed as female.

In much of this literature, certain specific character traits tend to be associated with each model. The characteristics associated with the traditional leadership model, for example, include aggression, domination, intimidation, and emotionless rigidity (Applebaum and Shapiro, 1993).The hierarchical management structure that is so much a part of the presidential expression accompanies this model, as well as the reliance on images meant to convey a sense of complete power and authority. Hierarchy defines the relationships in the traditional model and is heavily influenced by the demands of management.

Viewed from the point of view of feminist theory, the corporate model makes assumptions based on socially constructed notions of gender. As one might expect, the effect of this is that it tends to reproduce the social constructions and the assumptions based on them: For example, the idea that women are not aggressive managers (Applebaum and Shapiro, 1993).The difficulty here is that not only is the traditional model heavily imbued with maleness and qualities associated with the construction of maleness, such as: leader as master, as competitive, and as exclusionary (Smith and Smits, 1994: 44), but it also has diminished the effectiveness of an increasingly diverse workforce that views this quality as axiomatic.

DE FACTO FEMINISM AND THE CORPORATE CULTURE

The presence of de facto feminists within the corporate world has transformed the corporate model itself. Briefly put, corporate America noticed the shortcomings of its previous models as a leadership style and took note of something else--the greater efficacy of the women within their corporations who exercised leadership or were in leadership positions.

It may be useful at this juncture to look more closely at an alternative model of leadership usually associated with so-called female qualities. First, this model of leadership is usually regarded as the "tranformational" or "interactive" model in the literature on leadership. It is defined as a style that "occurs "hen one or more persons engage with others in such a way that leaders and followers raise one another to higher levels of motivation and morality" (Tolleson-Rinehart and Stanley, 1994:143), and the characteristics associated with this "interactive" model include: team work, leading from within the group, interpersonal relationships, personal input, and approachability.

A flat or horizontal management structure accompanies this form of leadership. Specific examples of qualities connected with "interactive" leadership include:"leader as colleague," "influence through persuasion," "cooperation," "collectivism," and "inclusion" (Applebaum and Shapiro, 1993: 31). For the most part "interactive leadership" is a modern model of leading, and has resulted in part, from the praxis of de facto feminists within the corporation. While the interactive model of leadership was once criticized for its feminist style, it has now become popular in corporate America (Smith and Smits, 1994), for its appeal to changing realities in both the global economy and the diversified work force. It can also be distinguished by the fact that it reflects the importance of "power to" as group empowerment. This then becomes the practical meaning of women exercising leadership (Austin and Leland, 1991), and ironically, it has become a significant asset to achieving corporate goals. If capitalism is anything, it is accommodating, and as the patriarchal components of corporate leadership were viewed as inhibiting productivity, they have been jettisoned.

Traditionally, of course, within the corporate model the leader exerts command by way of dictates and relies heavily upon his or her position within the chain of command. As might be expected, there were corresponding personality traits to the patriarchal form of corporate leadership. Often this approach looked for traits as forecasters of successful leadership, and within the corporate environment it was not unusual to find the establishment of a battery of tests in order to determine the likely leaders within an organization. Needless to say, an entire panoply of ideology was developed to celebrate the lucky possessor of such "natural," patriarchal ability. Unfortunately, "natural" leaders proved not to be the best mix for accomplishing the contemporary tasks that corporate management expects of its leaders, such as managing with a diverse and shrinking workforce. So this has given way to a wave of interest within the corporate environment for alternative ways of leading. This helps to explain the corporate interest in imported models of leadership, especially those from the Japanese corporate environment, for instance *quality circles*. Many of these styles of leadership were gradually abandoned because of the social commitment that this style of management implied.

One lesson that we can discern from these models of leadership has to do with ontology. Specifically, as we have discussed in earlier chapters, it constructs the individual leader as separate from the community of which they are a part and from whom they derive their capacity to lead, or their legitimacy.

Patriarchy expresses itself in the leadership styles discussed here by the many pitfalls that become all too obvious when leaders fail. One of these pitfalls is the problem of "abstraction"--the problem of examining the parts of an issue outside of the overall context in which it is found-- as in the Japanese example we just cited. For example, importing the leadership model without the commitment to long-term employment which is a feature of Japanese culture. Placing an emphasis upon the traits or qualities of existing leaders without addressing the context leads to attributing certain characteristics to men and others to women.

Austin and Leland's analysis allows us to locate de facto feminists contextually, and it also allows us to view their contribution to leadership by using a categorized historical approach. They focus on three generations of women, whom they refer to as *instigators, predecessors, and inheritors*, but whom we recognize as de facto feminists, and who were leaders. In place of certain character "traits," they arrive at three distinct and historical forms of de facto feminist leadership which also indicates how each generation builds on the work of the previous one. The discussion is quite interesting when approached from the point of view of what has been said so far in this work about de facto feminism. For, as we will see, many of Austin and Leland's categories are discernable within the established framework of de facto feminism.

The three different categories of women may be viewed as addressing historical patterns of de facto feminist activity. For example, the *instigators* are women who assumed leadership roles in the 1960s and 1970s at the onset of what is sometimes referred to as the Second Wave of feminism. Prior to then, they use the term *predecessors* to describe women whose contribution to leadership was exercised through improving education for women and contributing to the overall development of women. The third category is that of *inheritors*, those who are the beneficiaries of these developments and who took leadership roles in more recent times.

Austin and Leland's analysis of the emerging model of feminist leadership notes the emphasis upon "process" and the idea of "leadership in action," as describing the practical element of this leadership style. However, it is in their discussion of leaders that they combine these aspects, all of which are antithetical to the patriarchal style. Instead, they emphasize the concept of empowerment in the emergent form. As they put it: "However, they [women leaders] used their position as a power base to influence and to develop networks that, in turn, became the powerful agents of change. By empowering others, they were able to create a collective that worked synergistically" (Austin and Leland, 1991: 119).

The leaders that Austin and Leland studied, both positional and non positional, emphasize the importance of process and action in such a way that leadership is not the end in itself, but is tied to specific attempts to redress social injustices, where the focus is not on the individual personalities of the respective leaders but is on the practical function of leadership. Praxis then, is also important in the analysis of feminist leadership because it underscores the ways in which individuals become leaders--through the previous praxis of "predecessors," and their own transformational praxis.

A praxis approach reconstitutes the very axes of leadership itself. Feminist praxis and leadership has a twofold, transformational effect upon both the vertical and horizontal axes of leadership. The first axis is one that we find in the corporate model of leadership that was discussed earlier--the *horizontal* axis of net relationships--the totality of which is referred to as one's network. For de facto feminists, the horizontal axis, the network of relationships is the ground of strength as well as their source of legitimacy. It replaces the "qualities" or "traits" of the individual.

The second axis--the vertical axis--represents the traditional "chain of command" structure. It is qualitatively different in the case of feminist praxis. In any of the earlier nonfeminist models the vertical axis is equated with, or in some cases synonymous with, hierarchy. However, for the feminists approach the vertical axis refers instead to levels of praxis, or what can also be referred to as levels of involvement within the wider feminist project. It is a notion of leadership that does not grant the individual a status apart from the community of which one is a leader. The leader needs to be in constant touch and interaction with their host community. I say this because if we revisit the lessons provided us by our analysis of women's history, and as that history is viewed by Austin and Leland in their generational account, then we see that women's history and the development of leadership is itself a community, apart from which we cannot even envision leaders.

What we find to be the case with regard to de facto feminist leadership is that the process of discussion, of communicating with others, is itself politically generative. The ability to link up the content of that discourse with a wider series of debates has been aptly noted by scholars of social movements. One can speak then, of these informal discourses as attempts to translate this historical experience into the language of the existing, wider community of feminism in the contemporary environment.

In contrast, many of the models used to represent contemporary leadership follow closely the organizational charts that correspond to the chain of command. As a consequence, graphic representations would employ either a hierarchy, with some form of a chain of command structure, or a flow chart to emphasize the movement of ideas and the execution of corporate or political directives.

The emerging de facto feminist approach, however, is based on praxis and can be characterized as a gestalt composed of a network of relationships, and, since communication with the community of which one is a leader is continuous, the axes of action and leadership would be continually open.

The dialogue, in short, as well as the relationships and political action, would always already be in process, or it would be, as we termed it earlier, relational. Changes and corrections, precisely because they grow out of the gestalt, would be antithetical to the mechanical lines of inputs and outputs that usually characterize leadership flow charts. One representation of this field then, would be one where the traditional axes of communication and action are a totality composed of gradations in an overall continuum of action. The mechanism by which transformation takes place in this approach is that of praxis. The keen sense of social justice that has often been the hallmark of feminist leaders is probably not reducible to a formula. However, the development of that sense of justice through an exposure to grievance starts a process of transformation that includes discourse and activity and that results in political praxis--the taking of certain steps and the taking of specific actions to address these conditions.

Working against the initial set of conditions one experiences changes oneself as well as the process, creating possibilities for leadership. As Austin and Leland note:

As activists, the Instigators, whether in leadership positions or as academic scholars, sharpened their commitment to social justice and learned the power of protest for bringing about change. Their passion for justice was also fueled by their personal experience of discrimination, rejection, belittlement, and pain as women. All of these experiences impressed on them the need for knowledge that could be central to changing social institutions. (Austin and Leland, 1991: 76)

Rhetoric is also transformed. The community-grounded leaders constantly have their rhetoric checked by the community and the reverse so that the realities of contemporary politics are accounted for. Given that, the function of rhetoric is far different from patriarchal models, where rhetoric is often nothing so much as an expression of force. Rhetorically, a leader, as Austin and Leland highlighted, needs to be in constant touch with the community, or maintain a continuing relationship.

In traditional forms of leadership, especially political leadership, the primary purpose of rhetoric is to persuade, or as it is often put, to "win" the argument. In this model, by contrast, the emphasis is upon education --to "explain" the justice of one's position. For if one has a "just" position, then one's primary objective is to "explain" it and point out the injustice in those that stand over and against a just claim. The advancement of the politics is not the sole provence of the leader, but instead this responsibility lies with the community.

The philosophical question that is raised by the analysis of leadership is whether or not this represents a gendered approach likely to give rise to one more round of binary constructs along the lines of sameness and difference. But, I would argue that we can think of it that way only if we approach as necessarily true the alienated condition of life in patriarchal society. If we view the alienated condition as the norm then our arguments will reproduce those dichotomies as alienated theory. However, if we view political society as alienated in the first instance, then de facto feminism specifically, and feminism generally, will bring about a regeneration of human existence from its dichotomous past. We may wish to think of some of the contributions of de facto feminism and ask what is the norm? And, have we been well served by it? Which is to be preferred: sensitive, communicative and involved fathers? Or, authoritarian ones? Decision making that reflects a plurality of perspectives and anticipates likely problems? Or, ones that proceed full speed ahead, oblivious to all consequences except the accomplishment of the goal?

Eric Fromm once noted that politics in the late twentieth century could be characterized by the fact that authority and power are no longer exercised through the explicit use of force. Instead, he noted, it operates through the internalized social control, the end result of which is a certain hegemony over social reality. I have attempted to show how the activities of de facto feminists confront one important feature of that social control--that of patriarchy. The focus on praxis has allowed us to bring into relief the way in which de facto feminism has undermined patriarchal ideology.

NOTE

1. For additional analysis of this point, see Misciagno, "Rethinking the Mythic Presidency," in *Political Communication*, vol. 13, no. 3 (July-September, 1996).

Bibliography

Aisenberg, Nadya and Mona Harrington. *Women of Academe: Outsiders in the Sacred Grove*. Amherst: University of Massachusetts Press, 1988.

Andersen, Kristi. "Working Women and Political Participation, 1952-1972."*American Journal of Political Science*, 19 (1975), 439-453.

Applebaum, Stephen, and Barbara Shapiro, "Why Can't Men Lead Like Women?" *Leadership and Organizational Development Journal*, Vol.14 (7), 1993.

Arendt, Hannah. *The Life of the Mind*. New York: Harcourt, Brace, Jovanovich, 1978.

Austin, Helen S. and Carole Leland. *Women of Influence, Women of Vision; A Cross Generational Study of Leaders and Social Change*. San Francisco: Jossey-Bass, 1991.

Avis, Elizabeth Gold. *The First Sex*. Baltimore, Md.: Penguin Books, 1971.

Bacchi, Carol Lee. *Same Difference; Feminism and Sexual Difference*. Boston: Allen and Unwin, 1990.

Baer, Ellen D. "The Feminist Disdain for Nursing." *New York Times* (11 March 1991), op-ed page.

Baillie, J. B. *The Origin and Significance of Hegel's Logic*. New York: Macmillan, 1901.

Ball, Terence, ed. *Political Theory and Praxis: New Perspectives*. Minneapolis: University of Minnesota Press, 1977.

Baxter, Sandra, and Marjorie Lansing. *Women and Politics*. Ann Arbor: University of Michigan Press, 1983.

Bell, Susan G., ed. *Women, the Family and Freedom: The Debate in Documents*. Stanford: Stanford University Press, 1983.

Benhabib, Seyla and Drucilla Cornell. *Feminism as Critique*. Minneapolis: University of Minnesota Press, 1987.

Bergmann, Barbara R. *The Economic Emergence of Women*. New York: Basic Books, 1986.

Berlin, Isaiah. *The Crooked Timber of Humanity*. New York: Knopf, 1991.

Bernstein, Richard. "Hannah Arendt: The Ambiguities of Theory and Practice," Terrence Ball, ed., *Political Theory and Practice: New Perspectives*. Minneapolis: University of Minnesota Press, 1977.

Black, Naomi. *Social Feminism*. Ithaca, N.Y.: Cornell University Press, 1989.

Bookman, Ann, and Sandra Morgan, eds. *Women and the Politics of Empowerment*. Philadelphia: Temple University Press, 1988.

Bosworth, Stephen C. *Hegel's Political Philosophy*. New York: Garland, 1991.

Boxer, Marilyn. *Socialist Woman*. New York: Elsevier Press, 1978.

Braverman, Harry. *Labor and Monopoly Capital*. New York: Monthly Review Press, 1974.

Bunch, Charlotte. *Building Feminist Theory*. New York: Longman, 1981.

Butler, Judith. "Imitation and Gender Insubordination." In *Inside Out; Lesbian Theories, Gay Theories*. New York: Routledge, 1991.

Carroll, Susan J. "The Personal is Political: The Intersection of Private Lives and Public Roles Among Women and Men in Elective and Appointive Office." *Women & Politics*, 9 (1989).

-----. "Women's Autonomy and the Gender Gap: 1980-1982." In *The Politics of the Gender Gap*. Newbury Park, CA: Sage, 1990.

Castro, Ginette. *American Feminism: A Contemporary History*. New York: New York University Press, 1990.

Chafe, William H. *The Paradox of Change*. New York: Oxford University Press, 1991.

-----. *Women and Equality*. New York: Oxford University Press, 1977.

Conover, Pamela. "Feminists and the Gender Gap." *Journal of Politics*, 50 (1985).

Conrath, Cynthia. "Fearing and Denouncing Feminism," *Tapestry* (Winter, 1990), Bucknell Publications.

Cook, Adell. "Measuring Feminist Consciousness." *Women & Politics*, 9, no.3 (1989).

Costain, Anne N., "Representing Women: The Transition from Social Movement to Interest Group," *Western Political Quarterly*, Dec., 1980.

-----. "Women's Claims as a Special Interest." In Carol M. Mueller, ed. *The Politics of the Gender Gap*. Newbury Park: Sage, 1990.

Cott, Nancy F. *The Grounding of Modern Feminism*. New Haven: Yale University Press, 1987.

-----. *Root of Bitterness*. New York: Dutton & Co, 1972.

Dabrowski, Irene J. "The Unnamed Political Women." In *Women Leaders in Contemporary US Politics*. LeVeness and Sweeney, eds. Boulder, CO: Rienner, 1987.

DeBeauvoir, Simone. *The Second Sex*. New York: Bantam Books, 1964.

DeLauretis, Teresa. *Feminist Studies/Critical Studies*. Bloomington: Indiana University Press, 1986.

Delmar, Rosalind. "What is Feminism." In *What is Feminism*. Juliet Mitchell and Ann Oakley, eds. New York: Pantheon, 1986.

Delphy, Christine. *Close to Home: A Materialist Analysis of Women's Oppression*. Amherst: University of Massachusetts Press, 1984.

Deutchman, Iva Ellen. "Feminist Theory and the Politics of Empowerment." In *Women in Politics; Outsiders or Insiders?* Lois Lovelace, ed., Englewood Cliffs: Prentice Hall, 1993.

Dietz, Mary G. "Context is All: Feminism and Theories of Citizenship." *Daedalus*, 116 (1987).

Dionne, E. J. "Women's Lives: A Scorecard of Change," *New York Times Supplement to APSA*. 1989.

Donahue, Jesse. "Movement Scholarship and Feminism in the 1980s." *Women and Politics*, vol. 16, no. 2 (1996).

Donovan, Josephine. *Feminist Theory: The Intellectual Traditions of American Feminism*. New York: Ungar, 1985.

Dubois, Ellen Carol. *Elizabeth Cady Stanton*. New York: Schocken Books, 1981.

Eagleton, Terry. *Ideology*. New York: Verso, 1991.

Edmond, Wendy, and Suzie Fleming. *All Work and No Pay*. Bristol, England: Falling Wall Press, 1975.

Eisenstein, Hester. *Contemporary Feminist Thought*. Boston: Hall & Co., 1983.

Eisenstein, Zillah R. *Capitalist Patriarchy and the Case for Socialist Feminism*. New York: Monthly Review Press, 1979.

-----. *The Female Body and the Law*. Berkeley: University of California Press, 1988.

-----. *The Radical Future of Liberal Feminism*. New York: Longman, 1981.

Elshtain, Jean Bethke. *The Family in Political Thought*. Amherst: University of Massachusetts Press, 1982a.

-----. "Feminism, Family and Community." *Dissent*. (Fall 1982b), 442-450.

Evans, Judith et al., eds. *Feminism and Political Theory*. London: Sage, 1986.

Eyerman, Ron, and Andrew Jamison. *Social Movements; A Cognitive Approach*. University Park: Pennsylvania State University Press, 1991.

Faludi, Susan. *Backlash; the Undeclared War Against Women*. New York: Crown, 1991.

Farnham, Christie, ed. *The Impact of Feminist Research in the Academy*. Indianapolis: University of Indiana Press, 1987.

Ferree, Myra Marx and Beth B. Hess. *Controversy and Coalition*. Boston: Twayne, 1985.

Fierman, Jaclyn. "Why Women Still Don't Hit the Top." *Fortune* (30 July 1990).

Figes, Eva. *Patriarchal Attitudes*. Greenwich: Fawcett, 1970.

Firestone, Shulamith. *The Dialectic of Sex*. New York: Bantam Books, 1971.

Flexner, Eleanor. *Century of Struggle*. Cambridge: Harvard University Press, 1959.

Foucault, Michel. "About the Beginnings of the Hermeneutics of the Self; Two Lectures at Dartmouth." Mark Blasius ed., In *Political Theory,* vol. 21, no. 2, May 1993.

Fowkes, Diane. "Conceptions of the Political: White Activists in Atlanta." In *Political Women*. Janet Fleming, ed., Newbury Park: Sage, 1989.

Fox-Genovese, Elizabeth. *Feminism Without Illusions*. Chapel Hill: University of North Carolina, 1991.

Fraser, Nancy. "After the Family Wage: Gender Equity and the Welfare State." *Political Theory,* vol. 22, no. 4 (Nov. 1994).

----. "What's Critical About Critical Theory? The Case of Habermas and Gender," In *Feminist Interpretations and Political Theory*. Mary Lyndon Shanley and Carole Pateman eds., University Park: Penn State Press, 1991.

Friedan, Betty. *The Feminine Mystique*. New York: Dell, 1963.

Fromm, Eric. *Beyond the Chains of Illusion; My Encounter With Marx and Freud*. New York: Simon and Schuster, 1962.

-----. *Escape from Freedom*. New York: Anchor, 1968.

Gelb, Joyce and Marian Palley. "Women and Interest Group Politics." *Journal of Politics*, 41 (1978), 362-392.

Gelb, Joyce. Women and Public Policies. Princeton: Princeton University Press, 1982.

Gerson, Kathleen."Emerging Social Divisions Among Women: Implications for Welfare State Politics." *Politics & Society*, 15, no.2 (1986-87), 207-212.

-----. *Hard Choices*. Berkeley: University of California Press, 1985.

Gilligan, Carol. *In a Different Voice*. Cambridge: Harvard University Press, 1982.

Gould, Carol C. *Rethinking Democracy*. New York: Cambridge University Press, 1988.

Greer, Germaine. *The Female Eunuch*. New York: McGraw Hill, 1971.

Griffin, Fredrick, ed. *Woman as Revolutionary*. New York: Times Mirror, 1973.

Guettel, Charnie. *Marxism and Feminism*. Toronto: Women's Educational Press, 1974.

Gurin, Patricia. "Women's Gender Consciousness." *Public Opinion Quarterly*, 49, (1986), 143-163.

Hagen, Elisabeth, and Ceallaigh Reddy, eds. *Feminization of the Labor Force; Paradoxes and Promises*. New York: Oxford, 1988.

Harding, Sandra, ed. *Feminism and Methodology*. Bloomington: Indiana University Press, 1987.

Hartman, Heidi. "The Historical Roots of Occupational Segregation." *Signs,* Vol.1, (Spring, 1976), 137-169.

Hartmann, Susan M. *From Margin to Mainstream*. New York: Knopf, 1989.

Hartsock, Nancy C. M. *Money, Sex and Power: Towards a Feminist Historical Materialism*. New York: Longman, 1983.

Hegel, Georg. *The Phenomenology of Mind*. New York: Harper Colophon, 1967.

-----. *Reason in History*. Robert Hartman tr. New York: Bobbs-Merrill, 1953.

-----. *Science of Logic*. New York: Humanities Press, 1969.

Hewlett, Sylvia Ann. *A Lesser Life: The Myth of Women's Liberation in America*. New York: W. Morrow, 1986.

Hirsch, Marianne, and Evelyn Fox Keller. *Conflicts in Feminism*. New York: Routledge, 1990.

Humm, Maggie. *The Dictionary of Feminist Theory*. Columbus: Ohio State University Press, 1990.

Ibsen, Henrik. *A Doll's House*. New York: Modern Library, 1935

Jaggar, Alison M. *Feminist Politics and Human Nature*. Totowa: Rowman, 1983.

Jaspers, Karl. *Philosophy, Vol 2*. Chicago: University of Chicago Press, 1970.

Kamen, Paula. *Feminist Fatale*. New York: Donald Fine, 1991.

Kaplan, Cora. *Sea Changes: Essays on Culture and Feminism*. London: Verso, 1986.

Kelly, Rita Mae, and Jayne Burgess. "Gender and the Meaning of Power and Politics." *Women & Politics*, vol.9, no.1, (1989), 47-82.

Keohane, Nannerl, et al., eds. *Feminist Theory: A Critique of Ideology*. Chicago: University of Chicago Press, 1982.

Klein, Ethel. *Gender Politics*. Cambridge, Mass.: Harvard University Press, 1984.

Klein, Viola. *The Feminine Character*. Chicago: University of Illinois Press, 1971.

Kosik, Karel. *Dialectics of the Concrete*. Boston: D. Reidel, 1976.

Kramarae, Cheris. *A Feminist Dictionary*. Boston: Pandora Press, 1985.

Kruks, Sonia. *Situation and Human Existence: Subjectivity and Society*. NewYork: Unwin Hyman, 1990.

Lauer, Quentin, S.J. *Essays in Hegelian Dialectic*. New York: Fordham University Press, 1977.

Lerner, Gerda. *The Creation of Patriarchy*. New York: Oxford University Press, 1986.

Lifton, Robert Jay. "Protean Man." In *The Existential Mind*. Frederick Karl and Leo Hamalian, eds. Greenwich: Fawcett, 1974.

Lorber, Judith, and Susan A. Farrell, eds. *The Social Construction of Gender*. Newbury Park: Sage, 1991.

Lowi, Ted J. *The End of Liberalism*. New York: W. W. Norton, 1969.

-----. *The Personal President; Power Invested, Promises Unfulfilled*. Ithaca: Cornell University Press, 1985.

Lukacs, Georg. *History and Class Consciousness*. Rodney Livingstone, tran. Cambridge: MIT Press, 1976.

MacKinnon, Catharine A. "Feminism, Marxism, Method and the State: Agenda for Theory." *Signs*, vol.7, no.3, (1983a), 515-544.

-----. "Feminism, Marxism, Method and the State: Towards a Feminist Jurisprudence." *Signs*, Vol.8, no.4, (1983b), 635-658.

-----. *Feminism Unmodified*. Cambridge: Harvard University Press, 1987.

-----. "Legal Perspectives on Sexual Difference," In *Theoretical Perspectives on Sexual Difference*. Deborah L. Rhode, ed. New Haven: Yale University Press, 1990.

Mansbridge, Jane J. *Beyond Adversary Democracy*. New York: Basic Books, 1980.

-----. "Myth and Reality: The ERA and the Gender Gap in the 1980 Election," *Public Opinion Quarterly*, 49, (1985), 164-178.

-----. "The Role of Discourse in the Feminist Movement," Paper presented at the American Political Science Association meeting, Washington, D.C., 1993.

Marcuse, Herbert. *Between Luther and Popper*. New York: Verso, 1983.

Margolis, Diane Rothbard. "Considering Women's Experience: A Re-formulation of Power Theory," *Theory and Society*, 18 (1989).

Marilley, Suzanne M. "Towards a New Strategy for the ERA: Some Lessons from the American Woman Suffrage Movement," *Women and Politics*, 9(4) (1989).

Marshall, Susan E. "Who Speaks for American Women: The Future of Anti-feminism in Twentieth-Century America," *The Annals of the American Academy of Political and Social Science* (May 1991), 50

Marx, Karl. *Capital*. New York: International Publishing, 1977.

-----. *Grundrisse*. Martin Nicolaus, tran. New York: Penguin, 1993.

-----."Estranged Labor." In *The Economic and Philosophic Manuscripts of 1844*. Dirk J. Struik, ed. New York: International Publishing,1904.

Merleau-Ponty, Maurice. *Phenomenology of Perception*. Colin Smith, tran. London: Routledge, 1962.

Millett, Kate. *Sexual Politics*. New York: Avon Books, 1970.

Miner, Valerie, and Helen E. Lonqino, eds. *Competition: A Feminist Taboo?* New York: The Feminist Press, 1987.

Mitchell, Juliet, and Ann Oakley. *What is Feminism?* New York: Pantheon, 1986.

Mitchell, Juliet. *Women's Estate*. New York: Vintage Books, 1971.

-----. *Women, the Longest Revolution*. New York: Pantheon, 1984.

Morgan, Elaine. *The Ascent of Woman*. New York: Bantam Books, 1972.

Mueller, Carol M., ed. *The Politics of the Gender Gap: The Social Construction of Political Influence*. Newbury Park, CA: Sage, 1990.

Murray, Connie. "Ecofeminism: Gender and Support for Environmental Issues." Delivered at the August 1989 APSA Convention in Atlanta.

Myres, Sandra L. *Westering Women and the Frontier Experience 1800-1915*. Albuquerque: University of New Mexico Press, 1982.

Nickels, Elizabeth, and Laura Ashcraft. *The Coming Matriarchy*. New York: Berkeley Books, 1982.

Oakley, Ann. *Subject Women*. New York: Pantheon Books, 1981.

-----. *Women's Work*. New York: Pantheon Books, 1974.

O'Brien, Mary. *The Politics of Reproduction*. Boston: Routledge & Kegan, 1981.

O'Faolion, Julia, ed. *Not in God's Image*. New York: Harper and Row, 1973.

Ollman, Bertell. *Alienation; Marx's Concept of Man in Capitalist Society*. Cambridge: Cambridge University Press, 1978.

O'Neill, William L. *Everyone Was Brave*. Chicago: Quadrangle Books, 1969.

Peterson, Houston, ed. *Essays in Philosophy*. New York: Washington Square Press, 1974.

Phillips, Anne. *Engendering Democracy*. University Park: Penn State University Press, 1991.

Poster, Mark. *Existential Marxism in Postwar France: From Sartre to Althusser*. Princeton: Princeton University Press, 1982.

Rabinow, Paul, ed. *The Foucault Reader*. New York: Pantheon, 1984.

Rapp (Reiter), Rayna, ed. *Towards an Anthropology of Women*. New York: Monthly Review Press, 1975.

-----. "Family and Class in Contemporary America." *Rethinking the Family*. New York: Longman, 1982.

Riley, Denise. *Am I that Name?* Minneapolis: University of Minnesota Press, 1988.

Rix, Sara E. *The American Woman 1990-91: A Status Report*. New York: Norton, 1990.

Roelofs, H. Mark. *Ideology and Myth in American Politics*. Boston: Little, Brown, 1976.

-----. *The Poverty of American Politics*. Philadelphia: Temple University Press, 1992.

Rossi, Alice S. "Beyond the Gender Gap: Women's Bid for Political Power," *Social Science Quarterly*, 64, (1983), 718-733.

Rousseau, Jean Jacques. *The Social Contract and Discourses*. G.D.H. Cole tran. New York: Dutton, 1950.

Rowbotham, Sheila. *Women, Resistance and Revolution*. New York: Vintage Books, 1974.

Sartre, Jean Paul. *The Critique of Dialectical Reason*. New York: Vantage, 1972.

Sayers, Janet. *Biological Politics: Feminist and Anti-Feminist Perspectives*. New York: Tavistock, 1982.

Schattschneider, E. E. *The Semisovereign People*. New York: Holt, Rinehart and Winston, 1956.

Schneir, Miriam, ed. *Feminism: The Essential Historical Writings*. New York: Vintage Books, 1972.

Schurmann, Reiner. *Meister Eckhart Mystic and Philosopher*. Bloomington: Indiana University Press, 1978.

----. *Heidegger on Being and Acting; From Principles to Anarchy*. Bloomington: Indiana University Press, 1987.

Scott, Joan W. *"Deconstructing Equality-Versus-Difference: Or, the Uses of Poststructuralist Theory for Feminism."* In *Conflicts in Feminism*. Marianne Hirsch and Evelyn Fox Keller, eds. New York: Routledge, 1990.

Shanley, Mary Lyndon, and Carole Pateman, eds. *Feminist Interpretations and Political Theory*. University Park: Penn State University Press, 1991.

Shortridge, Barbara Gilma. *Atlas of American Women*: New York: Macmillan, 1987.

Sidel, Ruth. *On Her Own: Growing Up in the Shadow of the American Dream*. New York: Penguin, 1990.

Siegal, Roberta, and Lauren Burnbaum. "The Not-Me-Syndrome." Paper delivered at the 1989 APSA Convention in Atlanta.

Smith Patricia L., and Stanley J. Smits. "The Feminization of Leadership," *Journal of Training and Development*. February, 1994.

Snitow, Ann. "Basic Divisions in Feminism," *Dissent*, Spring, 1989.

----. "A Gender Diary." In *Conflicts in Feminism*. Marianne Hirsch and Evelyn Fox Keller, eds., New York: Routledge, 1990.

Sokoloff, Natalie J. *Between Money and Love*. New York: Praeger, 1980.

Spelman, Elizabeth V. *Inessential Woman; Problems of Exclusion in Feminist Thought*. Boston: Beacon Press, 1988.

Stacey, Judith. "Are Feminists Afraid to Leave Home?" In *What is Feminism?* Juliet Mitchell and Ann Oakley, eds. New York: Pantheon, 1982.

Staggenborg, Suzanne."Organizational and Environmental Influences on the Development of the Pro-Choice Movement," *Social Forces*, 68 (1989).

Stanley, Liz. "British Feminist Histories: An Editorial Introduction," *Women's Studies International Forum*, 13 (1990).

Stanton, Elizabeth Cady. *Eighty Years and More: Reminiscences, 1815-1897*. New York: Unwin, 1898.

Steinem, Gloria. *Outrageous Acts and Everyday Rebellions*. New York: Holt Reinhart and Winston, 1983.

Thorne, Barrie, and Marilyn Yalom, eds. *Rethinking the Family*. New York: Longman, 1982.

Tolleson-Rinehart, Sue, and Jeanie R. Stanley. *Claytie and the Lady*. Austin: University of Texas Press, 1994.

Tong, Rosemarie. *Feminist Thought*. Boulder, CO: Westview Press, 1989.

Trahey, Jane. *Women and Power*. New York: Avon Books, 1970.

Weed, Elizabeth. *Coming to Terms*. New York: Routledge, 1989.

Wolf, Naomi. *The Beauty Myth*. New York: W. Morrow, 1991.

Wollstonecraft, Mary. *A Vindication of the Rights of Women*. New York: W. W. Norton, 1967.

Wright, Erik Olin. "Women in the Class Structure." *Politics & Society*, 17, no.1, (1989): 35-66.

Zaretsky, Eli. *Capitalism, the Family and Personal Life*. New York: Harper Colophon Books, 1976.

Index

About the Author

PATRICIA S. MISCIAGNO is Assistant Professor of Political Science at Manhattanville College. She has written previously on Women and Politics and the American Presidency. She is currently at work on a book on the philosophy of social movements in America.

ISBN 0-275-95825-6

HARDCOVER BAR CODE